"A gaping hole in the literature of youth and young adult ministry has been a book on college ministry, as college and university life is currently experienced by young people. Chuck Bomar has ably filled that gap with *College Ministry 101*. Conversant with the latest thinking in late adolescent (i.e., college-age) developmental theory, and honed by years of work with university students, Chuck's book will be the gold standard in this area for many years to come."

—Tony Jones (tonyj.net), author, *The New Christians: Dispatches from the Emergent Frontier*

"For too long, college ministry has been a black hole of uncertainty and ambiguity. I have great respect for Chuck Bomar and love how his book shines light on the whys and hows of college ministry."

—Kara Powell, executive director, Fuller Youth Institute

"I've known Chuck for many years and this book isn't just theory; It's filled with insight from someone who's been totally immersed in very fruitful college ministry. I'm so thrilled that this book has been written because it's urgent that we pay attention to the college age group and the uniqueness of it. I don't know of any other book that gives as much practical wisdom as this one."

—Dan Kimball, author, *They Like Jesus but not the Church*

"We've searched for years for a book that would help us to both understand and serve college students with the same energy and passion we provide middle and high school students. In *College Ministry 101* we now have not just a book, but *the* book. Chuck Bomar, a smart, gifted and seasoned pastor to college students and young adults, has taken what's made him the most sought-after college ministry trainers in the country and created the resource that will be the standard for years to come."

—Chap Clark, Fuller Theological Seminary

CHUCK BOMAR

COLLEGE MINISTRY 101

A GUIDE TO WORKING WITH 18-25 YEAR OLDS

youth
specialties

ZONDERVAN.com/
AUTHORTRACKER
follow your favorite authors

ZONDERVAN

College Ministry 101: A Guide to Working With 18-25 Year Olds
Copyright 2009 by Chuck Bomar

YS Youth Specialties is a trademark of YOUTHWORKS!, INCORPORATED and is registered with the United States Patent and Trademark Office.

This title is also available as a Zondervan ebook.
Visit www.zondervan.com/ebooks.

Requests for information should be addressed to:

Zondervan, *Grand Rapids, Michigan* 49530

Library of Congress Cataloging-in-Publication Data

Bomar, Chuck.
     College ministry 101 : a guide to working with 18-25 year olds / by Chuck Bomar.
       p. cm.
     Includes bibliographical references and index.
     ISBN 978-0-310-28547-2 (softcover)
     1. Church work with youth. 2. College students—Religious life. I.
    Title. II. Title: College ministry one hundred one. III. Title: College
    ministry one hundred and one.
    BV4447.B66 2009
    259'.24—dc22   2009021656

Cover design: Toolbox Studios
Interior design: Brandi Etheredge Design

Printed in the United States of America

13 14 15 16 /DCI/ 23 22 21 20 19 18 17 16 15 14 13 12 11 10 9 8 7 6 5

ACKNOWLEDGEMENTS

I am grateful to so many people, but I'll mention the people who have directly influenced my thinking about college-age ministry. To Francis Chan, thank you for being so faithful in speaking truth into my life, being a loyal friend, and taking a chance on me. To the elders of Cornerstone, thank you for faithfully walking along-side me in joy, pain, and times of failure and success. To Todd Nighswonger, thank you for being such a dedicated friend and solid sounding board in every area of life. Thank you to everyone who served on staff with me in college ministry up to this point: Lara and Scott Mehl, Alison Davis, Joe Barsuglia, Chad Salstrom, Matt Moore, Tippy Littlefield, Suzy Hoekendorf, Stacy Leatherman, and Meagan Martin. Most of all I want to thank my wife, Barbara, for faithfully supporting me in every way possible—I love you very much. Lastly, thanks to my two daughters, Karis and Hope—I love you girls more than you'll ever know.

DEDICATION

This book is dedicated to those faithfully serving
college-age people.

CONTENTS

Appendices

INTRODUCTION

Much has brought me to the point of writing this book, but above all it's a concerned heart. I'm concerned about the number of high school graduates detaching from the church. I'm concerned about the generational gaps that exist in most churches and how we seem to accept them as a fact of life. I'm concerned about college-age people who are desperately trying to figure out life, yet have very little connection with mature Christian believers. I'm concerned that so few resources really get to the heart of college-age ministry. I'm so concerned about all of these problems that I can't sit back and wait for someone else to fix them. I want to do my part to change the shape of college-age ministry.

I'm so passionate about the church embracing college-age people that I've devoted a huge part of my life to helping churches understand how this ministry is vital for their context. After you read this book, I hope you won't just have a better idea about how a college-age ministry supports your local church or better understand how college-age people think, but that you'll also get a glimpse of God's heart for college-age people. You can know all the right stuff, but without love for God and God's people, all that knowledge means nothing.

College-age ministry is more than head knowledge for me. These students are real people, people who are graduating from high school and falling into damaging, dangerous ways of living because local churches don't walk alongside them. They're people who leave the church after high school and never come back. They're people who grew up loving God, seeking faith, and being willing to serve, but who've been abandoned by the church simply because they got older.

This book is my attempt to stop the bleed of college-age people leaving the church. But my goal isn't just to help the church. It's also to help the college-age people. Of course, I believe the church will benefit, but the first priority of a college-age ministry has to be the people themselves. As I'll say repeatedly in the pages that follow, college-age ministry has to be about relationships first. If it's about anything else, it's a waste of time.

Whether you've been involved in college-age ministry for years or are just getting started, the intention of this book is to help you discover what college-age ministry is—and what it isn't. The first section (chapter 1) is designed to give you a better understanding of why college-age people need a ministry of their own. If you're pushing against a church structure that doesn't see the point of creating a new ministry for this age group, the next chapter will give you the backup you need to make your case.

The second section (chapters 2 through 7) is designed to give you insights into the minds of college-age people, helping you understand how they think through five major issues: Identity, intimacy, meaning, pleasure, and truth. Knowing how college-age people process essential life questions in these areas is vital to effective discipleship. If you're running into brick walls with your ministry efforts, this section will give you another glimpse into what college-age people really need from you.

The third section (chapters 8 through 12) is designed to give you practical advice in the areas of leadership, teaching, your gathering time, working with volunteers, and most importantly, assimilating students into the adult life of the church. Figuring out the nuts and bolts of ministry can be a real challenge for those of us who prefer to focus on relationships. This section will show you why you don't have to give up one to be good at the other.

What you won't find in this book is a template for ministry. I won't give you program suggestions or ideas for big events. I won't offer how-to lists or recommend resources. Rather, my desire is to help you think through college ministry in your setting. My hope is that as you read each section, you'll find concepts that inspire you and ideas with which you disagree. I hope you can read this book, along with a few others, so you can process what you're reading as a ministry team and figure out what it means in your context.

I also hope this book encourages you as a leader. While plenty is here to help you with your ministry, I also know that leading a college-age ministry can be lonely and frustrating. As you read, I think you'll discover it doesn't have to be this way. College-age ministry can be life-changing for the people in your ministry, and it can be life-changing for you as well. You don't have to be a great speaker, an inspiring leader, or a big visionary to have an effective college-age ministry. You just need to love college-age people and be willing to invest in their development. This model of ministry might be completely different from what you're used to; but believe me, it's a model that's far more sustainable.

Most of all, I hope this book is the beginning of a very long discussion for you and others you know who care about college-age people. My prayer is that this book serves as a catalyst for many more books and resources that focus on church-based college-age ministry. Maybe reading these pages will even inspire you to write something of your own. In any case, I'm glad you've picked up this book. A world of college-age people needs someone like you to come alongside them as they grow into the people God created them to be. And I can tell you from experience, it's a true privilege to be that someone.

SECTION ONE
Unraveling the Myths

CHAPTER 1

WHY COLLEGE-AGE MINISTRY?

My friend Reggie and I were just sitting down for lunch at my favorite restaurant, getting ready for some great Greek food, when he told me the story of a girl named Nemo.

Nemo is a girl from Africa who had been sponsored through a well-known child-sponsorship ministry. Reggie explained that when Nemo turned 18, all the support she'd been receiving from the ministry stopped. He told me this procedure was normal for most organizations that provide this type of support. Nemo was going to be on her own, with no family to help her, no money to attend college, and no job experience. She was likely going to end up homeless once again, probably leaving her to heartbreaking ways of making ends meet. For her entire life, someone had made sure she had what she needed to survive. But once she was technically an adult, all of that support came to an end.

I was stunned. I bombarded Reggie with questions: How could something like this happen? How can an organization just drop people, leaving them with no hope? How many other kids like her were being moved out of a supportive network and abandoned to a life of theft, prostitution, and extreme poverty?

Reggie explained that the sponsorship organization had recognized this dilemma and developed a new program in which kids are sponsored all the way through college. It's a little more expensive because of the cost of a college education, but more help is available for these kids. This ministry saw the problem and created a way to fix it.

Can you imagine how we'd react if the executives of this organization had just kept going on as if this problem didn't exist? We'd question their motives and philosophy; we'd wonder whether or not they had the best interest of these kids in mind, or even if they were *truly* helping these kids. And yet we've let that same abandonment take place in our churches. We're not exactly leaving our high school graduates to lives of poverty and prostitution; but from a spiritual perspective, we're pretty close. We support our children until they finish high school; then we take that support away. We assume they'll transition, but they rarely do. After high school, many are left to figure out life for themselves. When the church isn't there for them, they look to the world for guidance.

Like that child-sponsorship ministry, the church must be willing to revisit the way we think about ministry in general, which means taking an unflinching look at life in our churches.

THE MESSAGE BEHIND THE METHOD

I've been known to make statements I've later regretted, but I don't think the statement I'm about to make will be one of them. I do need to preface it, however, with a few disclaimers. As a shepherd, I want what's best for the people in my care. As a pastor in a local church, I want what's best for the body as a whole. As a writer, I desperately want you to have the same passion and heart for both of those things as I have. That said, let me say this: One of the biggest challenges facing churches today is the loss of young people. And we church leaders have no one to blame but ourselves.

College-age people have been disconnecting from Christian community for far too long. Most churches seem to struggle with this issue, yet the pervasive lack of action suggests that they don't care as much as they say they do. Granted, more conversations about people's disengagement after high school are taking place than ever before, but this discussion should be *the* conversation going on in the church. Instead, when young people graduate out of student ministry, our actions scream, "We don't care about you anymore! You don't belong in our church! You're not important enough for us to spend quality time with you!"

I've spent the last decade working with college-age people and consulting with dozens and dozens of churches trying to find answers to the big questions of college-age disengagement: Why are so many people disconnecting after high school? As churches, are we making mistakes that contribute to this disconnection? What changes have occurred in society that so drastically affect people in this stage of life? What specific issues are college-age people dealing with that we're failing to understand or address? What can we do to engage the hearts and minds of people during this stage? This book is the result of asking those questions and working to find answers.

I want to be very clear about something right here at the start: My concern with the detachment of college-age people has nothing to do with having fewer people in our churches. If you're hoping to use college-age ministry as a church-growth tool, this book will be quite disappointing for you. Rather, the concern I have is strictly one of discipleship. Ephesians 4:11-13 describes the body of Christ as a means of discipleship. The church is meant for our growth, not the other way around. Paul writes, "So Christ himself gave the apostles, the prophets, the evangelists, the pastors and teachers, to equip his people for works of service, so that the body of Christ may be built up until we all reach unity in the faith and in the knowledge of the Son of God and become mature, attaining to the whole measure of the fullness of Christ." At the same time, if people detach from the body of Christ, they simply can't mature.

If our goal is to develop mature believers (and I hope it is!), we can't afford to watch college-age people detach from the church. Developing ministries that nurture and disciple college-age people isn't optional for churches. It's part of our calling as the body of Christ.

WHY WHAT WE'RE DOING ISN'T WORKING

I meet plenty of people who are doing their best to create college-age ministries. They plan big events and concerts, set up retreats and camps, design separate church services, or push for contemporary music in the service, all in an effort to draw college-age people to the church. Sure enough, college-age people show up for a few of these events or check out a church service. But they don't stick around; they don't engage. Once the novelty of the ministry wears off, they're on to the next thing.

The problem I see in most college-age ministries is that the leaders have their priorities out of whack. They start with the desired end result, rather than with the real needs of the people they hope to serve. Typically, when we start a ministry, the first thing we think through is how to get people to show up. We look at the ideas other people have implemented and figure out how they can work in our churches. We want to reach people—as many of them as possible. For so many college-age-ministry leaders, the goal is numbers. I know it was mine.

If I could've done anything differently in my work, I wish I would've put more thought into how this new ministry supported the overall structure of my church and the lifelong discipleship process of college-age people. Instead, I was concerned about how everything else in our church supported my ministry. I was concerned about getting people to come to our weekly gathering and making sure it was a great "experience"—achieving these two objectives was how I defined success for our ministry. I would've been much more effective in college-age ministry from the beginning had my priorities been in order—and more people might have gotten involved.

Any leader with a desire to create a college-age ministry needs to have a clear understanding of two issues: How this ministry fits into the church as a whole and what kind of discipleship college-age people need.

No matter what position you hold or how long you've been involved in ministry, you've probably noticed a great deal of disunity in churches. This problem affects not only the people who attend the church, but the church staff as well. One of the biggest reasons for this division is that people tend to lack an understanding of how their ministry supports other ministries in the church. We hire "professionals" in a particular area or department who come into a church context to use the resources of the church to build their ministry. There's no sense of one ministry flowing into another or even a sense of each ministry flowing into the life of the church as a whole.

The effective leader of a college-age ministry will be a true team player. I've helped many churches start college-age ministries, and I can tell you it's already a sort of "stepchild" in the church. Leaders of this ministry not only have to view college-age ministry as a part of the whole, but they often need to explain to other staff members why it's a key element in the overall structure of their church as well. If you don't know the answer to that question, stay tuned. I promise I'll show you what I mean.

The next section of this book will go into greater depth about the specific discipleship needs of college-age people. But before we get there, it's helpful to debunk one of the major myths about college-age people—that they're adults. Yes, they've reached the age of 18, and in a legal sense they are adults. But that technicality is really the only sense in which the word *adult* applies to college-age people.

Perhaps the most important discovery I've made is that to be effective in college-age ministry, we first must understand the world in which college-age people live. Being aware of their world has everything to do with who they are and what they need from a ministry. Even if you're only a few years out of this stage yourself, it's crucial to be a constant student of youth culture in this country. College-age people are bombarded with messages about who they should be and what they should do. By paying attention to the cultural shifts that shape them, we can see that now, more than ever, college-age people need faith communities to help them navigate their journey to adulthood.

Higher education. The pressure to go to college has never been greater. In a tight job market, there's no question that a college degree is now a necessity. Where high school graduation was once the first step into adulthood, it's now just a move from one kind of education to another. It has about as much significance as the move from junior high to high school. Since 1970, the number of 18-to-24-year-olds enrolled in degree-granting institutions has increased by 97 percent.[1] Nearly 40 percent of people obtaining a four-year degree plan to get a master's degree, and nearly 30 per-

---

1 National Center for Education Statistics (2004).

cent plan to take their education even further.[2] It's hard to feel like an adult when school is still the center of your day-to-day life.

Delayed adolescence. The view of college as an extension of high school means that the late teens and early twenties are viewed as a kind of extended adolescence. College means four more years of putting off "adult" decisions about work and family. Today, 13 percent of people between the ages of 25 and 29 are still in school. Compare that statistic with the percentage of 18-to-24-year-olds who were still in school in 1950—just 9 percent. These circumstances leave today's college-age people in the same position that high school students were in a generation or two ago—still in adolescence, preparing for adulthood.

Delayed family life. More and more college-age people are waiting until they earn at least a four-year degree and settle into a career before thinking about marriage or parenthood. In 1950, the median age of marriage for women was 20, and for men, 22. In 1970, the average age had risen to 21 for women and 23 for men, and as of 2000, the average age was 25 for women and 27 for men. College-age people now view adulthood as a time of stability. From an adult perspective, "stability" is great. But for a college-age person, marriage and family also mark the end of autonomy, spontaneity, exploration, and freedom. And they're in no hurry to let go of any of those liberties.

Financial dependence. Today, 73 percent of 18-to-25-year-olds get financial help from their parents. Even those whose parents don't financially support them tend to think their parents should. This fact is yet another indicator of delayed adolescence.

The post-high school years are no longer a time of independent adult life, but a stage that requires the care and nurture of

---

2 Arthur Levine & Jeanette S. Cureton, *When Hope and Fear Collide: A Portrait of Today's College Student* (San Francisco: Jossey-Bass, 1998).

older adults. Because of these issues, I'll refer to this stage as *late adolescence* and use the term interchangeably with *college-age*.

The extension of adolescence, combined with the historically unique demands in the workforce that require more education and the desire to hold on to independence for as long as possible, have created a new "age stage" of life. Young people go through a massive amount of change between the ages of 18 and 25. It's an extremely volatile time in life, and the church can provide much-needed stability.

I bet I can guess what you're thinking—because I get asked this question every time I speak about college-age ministry: Why go all the way to 25? The assumption is that a college-age ministry should end when college ideally ends—22 or 23 years old. But I believe it's far better to expand the age on the top end to make sure we're ministering to people all the way through this delayed adolescence. If you're not convinced, find a 24-year-old and ask her if she feels like an adult yet. If she's anything like the hundreds of 24-year-olds with whom I've worked in my years of ministry, the answer will be a resounding, "Not really!"

We have to recognize the years between 18 and 25 as a unique stage in life, a time in which people go through one of the most intense periods of change they'll ever experience. We can't treat them like children, but we can't treat them like full-fledged adults, either. They're in a stage like no other, which means they need a ministry like no other.

THE SOLUTION THAT ISN'T A SOLUTION

Plenty of churches have made a real effort to minister to college-age people. They've seen the detachment that comes after high school graduation and have worked hard to develop programs and services to help those college-age people stay connected to the church. Perhaps the most popular solution has been the "contemporary service" model that—while attracting some people from across generational lines—is intended to appeal to the late-adolescent and young-adult age group (18-to-35-year-olds). This service is meant to be a link between the structures that exist for children and those that exist for "adults." With an alternative service in place, the overall structure of the church looks like figure 1.1 below.

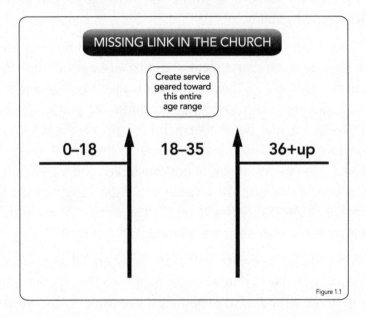

Figure 1.1

The strength of this approach is that typically a large number of people attend this service—often people who aren't attracted to the regular "traditional" service. But this approach has some real weaknesses as well. It rarely—if ever—involves assimilation strategies that serve as bridges to move people from one stage to the next. The model might delay detachment for college-age people for a few years, but eventually, they find that the separate-service model does very little to meet their actual spiritual needs. And frankly, it does very little to support the overall structure of the church—it doesn't address assimilation at all. A healthy college-age ministry supports the structure of a church by actively caring for college-age people while it helps them assimilate back into the overall life of the church.

Dan Kimball was instrumental in popularizing what was originally known as a "church-within-a-church" model. In this model, a ministry (such as Graceland, which Dan founded at Santa Cruz Bible Church) works within a church structure, yet in many ways functions as a separate church. In fact, Graceland eventually became a separate church. This progression is typical of effective ministries like this one.

While this model can be very effective, it does have one obvious downfall: Once the new church is planted, the older church is left with the original generation gap. A lot of churches are starting these types of services, but I'm not sure they always think through the implications of the model for their setting. The model itself isn't a problem—Dan has shown how beautiful this kind of ministry can be. But it's not the ideal solution for every church, particularly if the leadership doesn't think through the challenges very, very carefully.

Here are seven reasons why I believe the separate-church-service model of college-age ministry can create problems when it's used as a generic problem-solver, rather than an organic expression of the needs of the community.

1. **It rarely accomplishes what we think it will.** The hope for alternative services is that they'll help incorporate younger people into the broader church community. While it may be true that college-age people are gathering on the same campus or in the same building as the rest of the church, it doesn't mean they're incorporated into the church body. Just the opposite happens. College-age people are segregated, not

integrated. Granted, a separate service often attracts a large number of people, and those numbers can be very appealing to church leaders. But I find they hinder the creation of a unified and holistic church.

2. **It's overly focused on the church service.** This approach puts too much emphasis on the church service as a means of connection and discipleship. It also creates an environment where church attendance defines involvement. The point of assimilation isn't to make sure college-age people keep showing up on Sundays, but to help them engage in the life of the church—and in their faith—in deeper, more meaningful ways as they get older. When our structure suggests that a church service is the primary means of engagement, we'll inevitably lose college-age people.

3. **It can create teaching difficulties.** While it's true that you can't really miss when you preach to a broad audience, the flip side is that you can't really "hit" either. An 18-year-old and a 35-year-old typically have little in common—if they do, then bigger issues than assimilation are going on. These differences make it difficult to concentrate on intense late-adolescent issues that are such a huge part of discipling these young people. They have unique characteristics, and pinpointing them is vital for keeping people engaged.

4. **It can create division.** Even if this model were effective in the lives of college-age people, I'd find it troubling because of the chasms it creates between the generations. In its very nature, it tells everyone they have nothing in common with—and nothing to offer to—others in the church who fall outside of their age group or who don't share their musical tastes. Instead of helping everyone feel like they're part of the bigger mission of the church, this approach communicates the differences in values, not the

similarities. Having younger people gravitate to this alternative service leaves the church in the same predicament as before: College-age people aren't connected to the life of the church.

5. **It make discipleship more difficult.** The chasm between generations makes it difficult for people to follow the biblical mandates that older men (2 Timothy 2:2) and women (Titus 2:3-5) invest in mentoring young people. By focusing on the differences between the generations, rather than the similarities, this model makes it even more difficult to get older, more mature Christians to invest in the lives of college-age people. And it certainly doesn't make the old folks seem very appealing to the young ones.

6. **It can cause tensions between leaders.** Sadly, when these ministries succeed in reaching large numbers of people, they can become a point of envy between the senior pastor and the leader of the contemporary service. Leaders of the contemporary service can fall victim to their own egos, believing they'd be far more successful if they could get out from under the restrictions of the mother church. It's often these kinds of tensions that lead to a church plant, which again leaves the original church structure in the same predicament it was in before—being without a ministry to 18-to-35-year-olds.

7. **It's a temporary solution.** These services typically end up ministering effectively to one end of the post-high school age range while alienating the other. There are vast differences between 18-year-olds and 35-year-olds, and the ministry will eventually gravitate toward one end. These services usually begin as a means of attracting people on the younger end of the spectrum. But because no assimilation process is in place, no one wants to leave and start

over with the "old" people. So the ministry emphasis follows the crowd, and before long high school graduates feel left out and disconnected once again.

I believe this approach is a temporary fix, not a lasting means to assimilation. But up to this point, it has seemingly been the only intentional avenue for bridging the generational gap. My hope is to see churches embrace a different and lasting approach—college-age ministry as assimilation in the very best sense of the word.

THE REAL GOAL OF COLLEGE-AGE MINISTRY

Churches have a problem: High school graduates disconnect from the church, and far too many never come back. We're desperate for ways to keep college-age people engaged in the life of the church—not only for the sake of the church, but for the sake of these young people as well. We need ministries that bridge the generational gap between children and adults. No ministry will fill this need like a college-age ministry. Figure 1.2 shows the role a college-age ministry plays within a local church context.

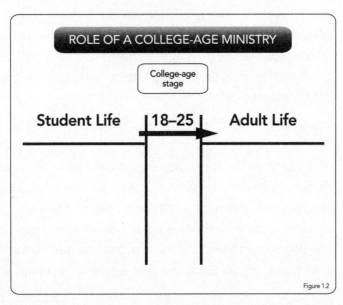

ROLE OF A COLLEGE-AGE MINISTRY

College-age stage

Student Life 18–25 Adult Life

Figure 1.2

The goal of a college-age ministry is to assimilate late adolescents into the body of the church (notice I didn't say *services*), with the ultimate goal being to produce mature believers who then live out the call of the faith. The good news is that churches don't need big budgets or separate services or huge events to achieve this goal. If we can meet college-age people where they are and guide them back into the life and body of our churches, we'll have done what we set out to do.

The years between 18 and 25 mark the stage of life when people are transitioning from a childlike dependency into mature independence. They have a foot in both camps but no solid grounding in either one. They're truly in between. College-age ministry fills a need in the lives of young people by walking them through the maturing process with love, care, understanding, and patience. What this ministry looks like will vary widely from one church to another; but if the mission is the same, we'll see a revolutionary change in our churches. We've seen it in our church. Our college-age people leave our ministry feeling sure of themselves, grounded in their faith, and most of all, essential to the life of our church. They don't just feel more comfortable; they know they belong.

College ministry is one of the most underutilized, underestimated, and underrated ministries in the church today because it's not understood. Local church leaders must see how this ministry supports the overall structure and maturity process of their people. Without a ministry to college-age people, both are stunted. If you want to be part of changing this dynamic, read on.

SECTION TWO
Understanding College-Age People

CHAPTER 2

THE UNIVERSAL IDENTITY CRISIS

Back in 2003, on a warm October afternoon, I sat outside my favorite coffee shop with Landen, a freshman at California State University, Northridge. I'd known Landen for a couple of years and had been discipling him as he made the transition from high school to college. As I drank my Pomegranate Blueberry Tea Latte (really, it's good), Landen told me about his college experience so far. It turned out it was exactly the opposite of what he'd hoped it would be.

Like most freshmen, Landen was excited about meeting new people and entering the next stage of life. But like so many freshmen, Landen was feeling detached from both his previous life and the life that seemed to be happening all around him at college. He wasn't sure who he was or how he fit in.

In high school Landen was popular, had a serious girlfriend, was president of the Christian club, and was a very good athlete. These affiliations didn't just keep him busy; they kept him feeling good about himself. All of this activity gave him a sense of identity. He was Landen—jock and all-around good guy.

Once he got to college, Landen began to feel isolated and alone. His friends had all gone in different directions after high school. Things didn't work out with his girlfriend. He was just one of many good athletes. His high school accomplishments didn't matter much at college, so he found himself starting over at square one, trying to figure out who he was, how he was different, and what his role in this new community might be.

Landen isn't alone in this search. This sense of detachment is a natural part of the transition into life after high school—you may have experienced this disconnect yourself. If so, you understand that when you lose a sense of who you are, all kinds of new questions come to the surface: Who am I? Where do I fit in? What makes me unique? What am I going to do with my life? This time of questioning and searching can be short and only mildly painful, or it can be so disorienting that a person ends up following all kinds of dangerous rabbit trails in an effort to find a place to fit in. One of the primary functions of any college-age ministry is to guide people through this search.

WHO AM I?

All kinds of theories explain identity formation. The best-known comes from a psychologist named Erik Erikson, who laid out eight distinct stages of development, starting with infancy and moving on through childhood, adolescence, and adulthood. Erikson's stages describe how identity is developed over a lifetime. While his ideas are immensely helpful, they can also be a little frustrating for those who work with college-age people and find themselves several stages down the road.

Another scholar, James Marcia, took Erikson's stages and broke them down into four specific states. According to Marcia, the typical adolescent shifts in and out of these four "states" of identity formation:

1. **Identity diffusion.** In this state, a person has no real sense of identity and no real desire to figure it out. She struggles with commitment and isn't searching for a sense of self.

2. **Identity foreclosure.** Many high school students are in this state. They have an identity, but it's based solely on the expectations and values of others—parents, friends, high school culture—rather than on their own exploration or values (again, no searching).

3. **Identity moratorium.** In this "identity crisis" state, a person is exploring his options but hasn't come to any conclusions about who he is and what he wants in life. It's a state with lots of searching but no commitment.

4. **Identity achievement.** In this state, the person finds a sense of identity. Her identity will still develop, but the basic understanding of who she is and how she fits in is in place. She demonstrates high commitment and is no longer intensely searching.[3]

I've found these four levels to be very helpful in understanding the process through which college-age people find a sense of identity. But both Erikson's and Marcia's work is limited to sociological and psychological perspectives. They don't include the spiritual element of the search for identity.

In my years of working with college-age people, I've used Marcia's categories as a foundation for what I've found to be five spiritually based stages in identity formation. I call them the Substitute, the Floater, the Explorer, the Tentmaker, and the Theologian.

---

3 James Marcia, "Identity in adolescence," in Joseph Adelson (Ed.), *Handbook of Adolescent Psychology* (New York: Wiley, 1980). Also see James Marcia, "The empirical study of ego identity," in Harke Bosma, Harold Grotevant & David De Levita (Eds.), Identity and Development (Newbury Park, CA: Sage, 1994).

Before I go into more detail about these stages, I want to say once again that identity formation isn't just a *big* issue for this age group. It is *the* issue. I know some leaders who wonder why they need to understand identity formation. They believe that if they simply teach the Word of God, then identity will take care of itself. But this search for identity is so all-consuming that it greatly impacts the way a young person understands the Word. Identity is where our concern ought to lie. It influences whether or not they'll take their faith seriously in the future. And if they don't embrace a clear identity during this stage of life, I dare say they probably won't embrace one at all. We can't effectively minister to college-age people if we don't meet them in the middle of their most profoundly life-changing experience.

This process makes more sense when we know a bit about the way identity forms prior to adolescence. Pre-adolescent children find their identity almost exclusively within the context of family. Other relationships—friends, neighbors, extended family—are in the child's life, of course, but even these relationships typically include a level of family involvement. As you know, this relational dynamic starts to change around the age of 10, when adolescent behaviors and attitudes start to kick in. Eventually, the child's life expands beyond the family to include more peer relationships.

If you've been involved in any kind of junior high ministry, you've watched this transformation happen. That nine-year-old who was afraid to leave his mom's side becomes the 12-year-old who doesn't want his mom to walk into the youth room to pick him up. As irrational as this behavior seems to adults, it's a necessary part of identity formation. In order for teenagers to become healthy adults, they must be able to function outside of their families. And that ability means looking to peers for cues on what's acceptable and what isn't.

During mid-adolescence (generally ages 14 to 17), identity is still formed through peer relationships, but a new influence—something I call a *social atmosphere*—has now entered the mix. A social atmosphere could be school, church, a sporting venue, home, a particular friend's house, or just about any place a teenager finds herself in the company of other people. Each social atmosphere has its rules and expectations for behavior, and 14-to-17-year-olds are particularly attuned to these rules and expectations. So a teenager has to make a series of decisions about how to fit in and function in these atmospheres.

For instance, a party requires certain characteristics and behaviors in order for a person to truly fit in and play an active role in the party. The requirements of the party are very different from the requirements of, say, a youth group meeting. Because the teenager wants to fit in and function in both social atmospheres, she adjusts her identity to fit the environment. True identity is substituted for what the atmosphere respects or requires. And that idea brings us to the first of my five states of identity formation in college-age people: The Substitute.

THE SUBSTITUTE: "IT MADE SENSE AT THE TIME."

Like the teenager shifting between his party persona and his church persona, the Substitute has yet to commit to a solid sense of identity. While this part of identity formation is typical for a mid-adolescent, it often continues well into the late-adolescent stage. Child-development expert David Elkind refers to this stage as a "patchwork self."[4] The Substitute is extremely susceptible to peer pressure and inconsistent behavior. He often makes decisions

---

4 David Elkind, *All Grown Up and No Place to Go: Teenagers in Crisis* (New York, NY: Perseus Books, 1998), 18-22.

that allow him to fit into one social atmosphere without truly understanding the implications of those decisions. Think about couples who get married right out of high school. They commit to a relationship in an effort to fit into a social atmosphere without really understanding what that commitment involves. The same is often true for college students who join fraternities or sororities in an effort to find an identity on campus. They substitute their own identity for that of the group. The social atmosphere has influenced a high sense of commitment, but the Substitute explores his personal identity very little outside of that context.

THE FLOATER: "I'M JUST WAITING TO SEE WHAT HAPPENS."

You know those aimless college-age people who just don't have a sense of direction? The ones who roam from part-time job to part-time job, or who have a different major every time they come home for break? Those are the Floaters. But Floaters aren't necessarily lazy or unfocused. They're in a normal developmental stage that often results from the pressure to do something with their lives. The response to this sometimes overwhelming pressure is to put off making that decision as long as possible—a total lack of commitment. Instead, the Floater lives day to day and puts very little thought into what might come next in life. You may observe hints that the search for a more solid sense of identity is still going on, but identity is primarily found in the person's current circumstances. The Floater isn't exploring identity as much as it might appear. Exploration takes intentionality and thought. It's a real effort to try on an identity and see how it fits. But the Floater isn't really looking for a fit—he's contentedly floating through life.

THE EXPLORER:
"I WANT TO KEEP TRYING DIFFERENT THINGS."

This stage is the opposite of the Substitute. The Substitute commits without exploring; the Explorer explores without committing. In my experience, most college-age people find themselves in this stage. They formulate their view of themselves primarily through relationships, school, and work.[5] But unlike the Floater, the Explorer is beginning to put more thought and intention into these parts of life. The Explorer is trying to find a major that will lead somewhere, dating with an eye toward marriage, and trying to work at jobs that have some connection to her life's dreams and goals. This level doesn't involve a fully realized identity, but it's a significant step toward developing one.

The Explorer stage happens when a college-age person develops the cognitive ability to go through a process Elkind refers to as "differentiation and integration."[6] Rather than making emotional and rash decisions—like the Substitute and the Floater—the Explorer engages in a conscious thought process that takes place over a period of time. And this process is essential to healthy identity formation.

Differentiation and integration begin as late adolescents start to place importance on the individual characteristics of people

---

5 See chapter 1 of *Emerging Adulthood: The Winding Road from the Late Teens through the Twenties* by Jeffrey Arnett. Arnett breaks these influences down into work, school, and love. However, it's not only in love relationships (i.e., dating) where identity is formed. Normal peer relationships also play a huge role and, in some ways, are even more influential.

6 Elkind, 18. Although Elkind doesn't limit this process to college age (late adolescence), he's clear that it's the healthiest way to formulate a sense of identity. He contrasts this stage with a substituted identity. The substituted identity is often formulated, or adapted, because the individual's abstract thinking hasn't yet developed to a point where he can walk through differentiation and integration. This underdevelopment leaves the individual with no choice but to adapt to different atmospheres, which Elkind calls "the development of a patchwork self." It makes sense that this person would be more susceptible to peer pressure because he lacks a sense of identity beyond the atmospheres in which he finds himself. Because this person has yet to think through who he is and how he may be different from others, he substitutes his true identity for that of his immediate context (i.e., circumstances in which he currently is). In my research, people who think through their identity at the Explorer level are typically college-age. I do believe adults can push high school students to think through these issues, but teenagers typically won't on their own. Also, they're less likely to make changes in their lives despite seeing contradictions in them.

and social atmospheres around them. They look at everything from the values and attitudes they see in others to the duties required for a job. Explorers assess all of this information as either respectable and desired or unsuitable and undesirable. They start to consider how they fit in with these people and atmospheres—and whether or not they personally *want* to fit in. Then they begin to differentiate and integrate. They differentiate the characteristics they see from those they believe they possess themselves. They pick and choose which characteristics they want to integrate into their identity and which ones they want to drop.

Obviously, this abstract cognitive approach demands a new level of self-awareness. And that self-awareness is self-perpetuating throughout this stage; the more the person differentiates and integrates, the more self-aware he becomes.

THE TENTMAKER:
"THIS IS WHAT I'VE ALWAYS WANTED TO DO."

This stage marks a balance between exploration and commitment. This person has gone through significant life experiences, which—coupled with her increasing self-awareness—gives her the ability to make concrete decisions about who she is. The Tentmaker tends to make choices that "click" with her as an individual because she's gone through the process of differentiation and integration. Because a conscious thought process preceded commitment, the Tentmaker is much more likely to withstand pressures from other people and social atmospheres and remain committed to who she believes she is.

For Marcia, this stage would represent "identity achievement." But I don't believe this marks the final stage for the college-age person. Marcia bases his sense of "achievement" on sociological achievement. He suggests that identity is settled when a person chooses a career, a relationship, and a living situation. Although all of these decisions point to a sense of stability, they'll almost always change. This stage is a tent, not a permanent home on a solid foundation, and it can be dangerous for a person to settle in this stage. Feelings of achievement come at this level; but if circumstances change, these feelings can turn to detachment and depression. The result is an endless cycle of crisis and shifting identity (see figure 2.1). That's why I've added another level of identity formation, one in which a person's identity moves beyond sociological markers.

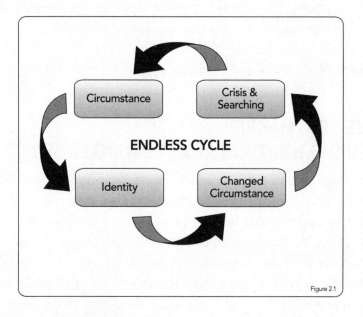

Figure 2.1

THE THEOLOGIAN:
"I AM A CHILD OF GOD."

Our job as leaders and ministers is to help college-age people move beyond the temporary tent of their circumstances. They need something more stable, more permanent. That fixed identity is what the Theologian stage is all about.

When I say *Theologian*, I'm not talking about a person who's been through seminary and is up on all the latest theological debates. I mean it in the truest sense of the word: One who studies God. Our deepest hope for the college-age people we work with is that they'll know God and live lives that honor God. And that hope will only be realized when they find their identity in him alone.

In grounding her identity in God, the Theologian takes what she's learned in the other stages and uses it to shape her views about who God has made her to be. Her identity is in him, not in sociological pursuits. Her relationships, job, and circumstances still matter. But instead of letting people and atmospheres define her, the Theologian wants her faith to define these relationships and experiences.

The Theologian will process her spiritual identity alongside her social identity. So as she moves toward an identity, she isn't just hoping to fit in or find her place in society. She has a mission mindset, one that inspires her to seek out roles in which she can live out her identity as a child of God (see figure 2.2).

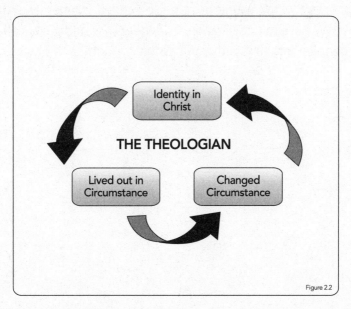

Identity in Christ

THE THEOLOGIAN

Lived out in Circumstance

Changed Circumstance

Figure 2.2

The Theologian can endure trials and changes in circumstances because circumstances don't define her. She finds meaning in something that doesn't change, no matter the circumstances.

Let's take a look at Landen's situation again. He lost the identity he'd found in the circumstances of high school life. High school provided a tent, but the storms of his post-high school transition had blown that tent over. When I met with him, he was searching for a new identity, something more grounded. He was firmly in Floater mode. He didn't have any sense of direction and wasn't sure where to turn for answers. His initial instinct was to try to find something in his new social atmosphere with which he could identify—a new girlfriend, a new sport, a new role on campus. At this point Landen could go in one of two directions to find an identity: Toward his circumstances or toward his faith. He had come to a fork in the road and needed someone to help him choose his path.

This moment of decision is perhaps the most important time in life. That's why college-age ministry is so important—not only to the young people we serve, but to the life of the church itself. We simply can't watch young people like Landen wander away from Christ. We have to understand this identity crisis and guide college-age people through it with compassion, wisdom, and prayer.

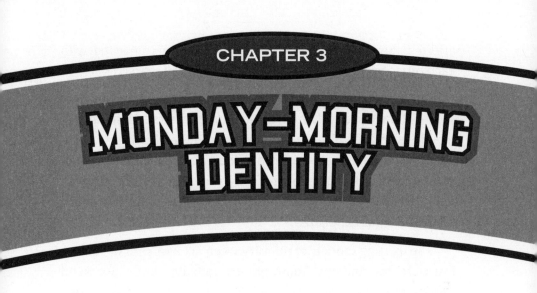

CHAPTER 3

MONDAY-MORNING IDENTITY

I often use the movie *The Breakfast Club* as a great example of the search for identity we see in college-age people. Each of the characters in this movie has a sense of identity prior to being inside the library that Saturday. There's the artsy girl with her dark clothes and withdrawn personality, the jock who always wears his letter jacket and is trying to please his dad by being a star wrestler, the popular girl dealing with the pressure to be cool and maintain her popularity, the rebel who's the clear product of an abusive father, and the academic nerd who has a good relationship with his family yet is completely disconnected from the social life of high school. They come to Saturday morning detention with different backgrounds, values, and identities that have been shaped long before they arrive at school that day.

But as the day—and the movie—progresses, a new social atmosphere is created, one that shifts the identity of each character. Each of them initially resists this shift, but by the end of the day, this new atmosphere—one in which honesty and vulnerability are respected and even required for them to function—has affected them all. As the movie ends, they've connected with each other by adjusting to the atmosphere they shared.

But imagine if the movie had shown us these same kids back at school on Monday. Maybe their connection would last the day, maybe even the week. But before long, these characters would likely fall back into their previous identities, the ones they use to function in the atmospheres they face every day. The commitment they had to honesty and vulnerability would vanish as quickly as it had appeared.

The existing models of ministry often act as a kind of "breakfast club" for students. Youth groups, retreats, camps, weekend conferences—these structures are all designed to create a unique social atmosphere in the hope that young people will find a new identity as "fired-up" Christians. But like that Saturday detention in the movie, this model can create a false sense of identity, one that can mislead leaders as well as students.

Let me use camp as an example of what I mean. I speak at a lot of camps, and I see the same thing happening everywhere. After a day or two, most of the students shift into a "camp" identity, one that reflects what's respected and required by this social environment. High school guys who would never be caught dead singing in front of their friends back home are eventually engaging in the songs at camp. Girls who take two hours to get ready for school will show up for a camp breakfast wearing pajamas and little, if any, makeup. Students join in activities they'd find silly and childish in the social atmosphere of high school. But at camp, silly is respected.

More importantly, faith is respected. The social atmosphere of camp requires and rewards faith engagement. It becomes normal and natural to have an identity in Christ. But unless the group leader knows how to help students transition back to their other social atmospheres, the faith identity that worked for them at camp will be replaced with whatever identity was working for them back home.

I don't mean to demean what God can and does do at camps, but my fear is that decisions and commitments made at camp (or youth rallies or concerts or retreats), although authentic in many ways, are too often made because those decisions were respected in that particular atmosphere. They're not conscious decisions born of true conviction. As leaders, we often create this "Saturday" atmosphere without preparing students for their "Monday" environments. The result is nothing more than a sub-stituted "Christian" identity. Christianity becomes a patch to be worn in certain atmospheres, one that's easily removed. We can help weave that patch into the fabric of our students' lives by naming what happens in a social atmosphere.

One of the parts of college ministry I enjoy most is the way the late-adolescent brain shifts into intense abstract thinking. A process that began in early adolescence is finally firing on all cylinders. This move from concrete thinking to abstract thinking means that leaders can engage college-age people on a far deeper level than would have been possible even a year or two earlier.

It's this cognitive change that makes it possible for us to have conversations about social atmospheres with college-age people. A 16-year-old might have a general grasp of the concept but not have the ability to do much about it in her daily life. A 19-year-old, how-ever, can not only understand the idea of a social environment, but she can consider the impact it has on her identity as well. So when we leaders talk about the effort we put into creating a particular social atmosphere at a camp or retreat, students get it. And when we talk with them about the difficulty of maintaining an identity that isn't dependent on social atmospheres, they get that, too.

I find that most college-age people long for that kind of identity. They don't like the feeling of shifting who they are to fit the situation. They want to feel confident in *who* they are, regardless of *where* they are. We can help them get there with six tools that I've found especially helpful in my work with college-age people.

1. KNOW YOURSELF.

First and foremost, those of us who work with college-age people need to embrace our identity in Christ. We have to be sure we have a sense of identity that goes beyond circumstances or vocation. If we don't, then the people with whom we're working won't either; we can only lead others as far as we've led ourselves. We don't have to have everything figured out, of course. But even being honest about our heart struggles and tensions in finding and embracing our identity in Christ can be a comfort and a guide to others.

2. FORCE THOUGHT.

I've learned that asking questions is a great way to help college-age people think through abstract concepts. I find that three questions in particular can help them—no matter which stage of identity formation they're in—move toward the Theologian stage.

Who are you? A guy named Scott approached me one night after our college-ministry group meeting. He told me he wanted to be in full-time ministry and wondered if I'd mentor him. I told him I'd be happy to, so we set a time to meet.

We started talking about his life at school, his girlfriend, his interests. Then I asked him, "Who are you?" Every time I ask this question of college-age people, I get the same response. It starts with a blank stare that screams, *I've never really thought about it before!* But they don't want to sound dumb, so they start telling me about their personality, interests, and activities. And every time I get that response, I reply, "So, that's what defines you?" Another blank stare.

I know it sounds a little devious to ask a question I know they can't answer, but I leave it ambiguous because I want to know how they view themselves. Their response tells me what kind of discipleship I need to be doing. It tells me how much thought they've given this concept. It gives me an idea of what stage of identity formation they're in and how much anxiety they feel about being in that stage. It also tells me where their faith factors in to their sense of self. For most, the answer is it doesn't.

The temptation at this point is to tell them what they need to do to find an answer to my question or to tell them they have to find their identity in Christ. But it's essential that I act as a sounding board for their efforts to find that answer for themselves. Most college-age people have spent their whole lives being told what to do and how to do it. The post-high school years mark the first time they've been allowed and encouraged to make their own decisions about what they do and who they are. As painful as it can be for them at times, figuring out who they are and what does—and doesn't—define them is a good, healthy, and even fun process. More intentional instruction may be necessary at times, but as a rule, leaders need to act as facilitators, not instructors. There's not one way for college-age people to figure out who they are. We have to help them find their own paths.

What are your strengths? This question is a big help for college-age people as they think about how they might fit into the world around them. I don't ask this question to figure out where a person can serve in ministry (although that may happen naturally), but rather to help move a person from a "What do I like to do?" mentality to a "Who has God made me to be?" mentality. And that transition eventually leads to the "What can I contribute?" mentality that's an essential part of moving into the Theologian stage.

Again, leaders feel a temptation to push college-age people toward an answer, especially if they can see particular ministry gifts in them. But we have to hang back and let them uncover these gifts for themselves. Our role is to help them discover who they are in Christ and how to live that out. Helping them make that self-discovery is a great joy of our role as leaders.

What makes you unique? This question allows us to walk college-age people through the process of becoming confident in how God made them. And that confidence is what helps them resist the pressure to let other people and atmospheres influence their identity. They're trying to figure out what independent adulthood looks like, and this small step of thinking about and embracing their uniqueness helps move them in that direction, whether in faith or vocation. Our role is to be their biggest fans—to encourage them, stand behind them, and cheer them on.

Late adolescents—like all of us—have a hard time intentionally focusing on their identity in Christ. But it's especially difficult for college-age people because their newfound freedom exposes them to a vast array of influences and experiences. They can easily get pulled back into previous stages of identity formation as they encounter new social atmospheres. Our role is to help them avoid that tendency by continuing to point them forward, toward the life they want to be living.

3. REVEAL YOURSELF.

In the previous chapter, we talked about the process of differentiation and integration. As you talk to college-age people, you'll discover they're looking to you for help in knowing what characteristics they should integrate. They'll often ask, "Who do you think I am?" or "What do you think my strengths are?" They want to know if your perceptions of them echo their beliefs about themselves. But they also want to figure out which parts you believe are valuable. They need you to reflect what's good, what's worth keeping, and what they need to let go.

These conversations are a big part of your role as a mentor and leader. But they can only happen if you make a real effort to be a person of transparency and authenticity. Coming across as someone who has it all together, who's never struggled with questions of identity, will just create a wall between you and the college-age people to whom you minister.

A recent study shows that people in their 20s are far more likely to reflect the values of their closest friends than the values of their faith.[7] I believe this dynamic happens because so few mature believers are willing to have honest conversations about life and meaning with college-age people. So they turn to their peers instead. And as 1 Corinthians 15:33 says, "Bad company corrupts good character." If we as the church fail to be real and honest with these young people, then we leave them little choice but to look to others for help during this significant life stage.

---

7 www.barna.org, October 31, 2006.

4. ENCOURAGE CROSS-GENERATIONAL FRIENDSHIPS.

College-age people are particularly tuned in to the specific character attributes and values they see in other people, making judgments about which values they want to integrate into their lives. Relationships with older Christians and exposure to their values are a crucial part of the process of identity formation. This fact seems especially true for churched kids coming out of high school.[8] The problem is that very few young people—as little as 25 percent[9]—actually connect with another Christian adult once they graduate from high school.

We leaders can't possibly be the only mature believers involved in the lives of college-age people. It's not healthy for us, for these young people, or for the church. So we need to encourage both our churches and the college-age people we work with to cross those generational boundaries and get to know each other! I'll provide more details on how to make this connection in chapter 12.

5. GIVE BIBLICAL GUIDANCE.

A person could argue that the whole of Scripture makes a case for finding our identity in God. But I find three passages in particular especially useful in talking with college-age people:

The book of Ephesians. Ephesians provides a perfect framework for understanding identity from God's perspective (chapters 1 through 3) and how we should live that out in our lives (chapters 4 through 6). Chapters 1 through 3 clearly articulate our spiritual

---

8 www.cyfm.net. For more information on what high school seniors desire, or to learn about research being done on the transition into college, see the College Transition link on this site. Research with 162 different seniors, all of whom are involved in the church, was still in progress as of March 2007, but it should be interesting to see how this project develops.

9 Kara Powell, *"Where do they go once they graduate?"* www.cyfm.net.

identity, and chapter 4 begins with the word *therefore*. Paul is essentially saying, "You are God's beloved child; that is your true identity. *Therefore*, here is how it should play out in your life." We become who we say we are by living life this way. Verses 4:1, 4:17, 5:1, 5:8, and 5:21 all begin sections that lay out concepts of living in light of our identity. Warning: Don't just jump to chapters 4 through 6! Make sure to talk about Paul's message on spiritual identity in chapters 1 through 3. Without that base, the rest can read as though it's focusing on behavior alone, rather than actions as the outgrowth of our identity in Christ. Skipping this crucial step can simply lead to a substituted identity in proper behavior.

Romans 7:14-25. College-age Christians often default to defining themselves by their sin. They can dwell on their failures with such intensity that it can be difficult to help them think of themselves in any other way. But God doesn't have this fallen view of believers (Ephesians 1:3-7), as Paul explains in Romans.

In this passage, Paul recognizes that he constantly does what he doesn't want to do and struggles to do what he *does* want to do. However, he *differentiates* his identity from sin. In verse 20 he says, "Now if I do what I do not want to do, it is no longer I who do it, but it is sin living in me that does it." The sin doesn't define him. He acknowledges his sinful tendencies (verse 24) but then speaks of his gratitude for Christ freeing him from sin (verse 25). He also recognizes that there is no condemnation for him (Romans 8:1) because his identity is found in Christ, not his sinfulness.

What would happen if we identified ourselves as holy and blameless (Ephesians 1:3-7) and completely apart from our sin? Would our lives be different? I believe so. We must help people differentiate their identity from the things of this world, including sin. Please understand, I'm not speaking of denying sin or not dealing with it. I'm talking about having an identity based on how God views us—as holy and blameless, "in accordance with the riches of God's grace" (Ephesians 1:7).

2 Corinthians 5:14-17. Paul explains that Christ's love compels him (verse 14), so he no longer lives for himself but rather for Christ (verse 15). Paul's description is a great picture of what life looks like for the person in the Theologian stage of development. Paul recognizes that he has a new identity, his old sinful self is gone, and he's been given a new purpose (verse 17). He lives in light of who he is from God's perspective.

I've found the best way to walk college-age people through these verses is to ask them to read the passages on their own, then discuss them together. I've also found that most college-age people haven't read much Scripture on their own, so they don't really know how to interact with the Bible. I have them interact with what they're reading by underlining ideas or phrases that stand out to them and then writing down any questions. When we can get college-age people thinking about life issues, show them that Scripture deals with those particular issues, and inspire them to study Scripture for themselves, we're on our way to true discipleship.

6. UNDERSTAND WHAT'S NORMAL.

College-age people find their identity primarily through relationships, work, and school. Each of these influences is so profoundly important in the life of a young person that I'll devote later chapters to a more in-depth discussion of each one. But details aside, it's important for those of us who work with college-age people to recognize that it's completely natural for these parts of life to take on tremendous importance for them. We need to acknowledge that importance and resist belittling them or dismissing the role they play in identity formation.

HOLDING UP THE MIRROR

I remember going to carnivals when I was a little kid. One of my favorite things was going into the house of mirrors. Some made you look really tall and skinny, and some made you look really short and wide. I was always amazed at the way these mirrors could distort my image.

What if those goofy reflections were the only image I'd had of myself? I'd have thought I was three feet tall and five feet wide! I wonder what kind of mirrors our college-age people are looking at? What kind of distorted view of themselves are they working from? And what happens when the only mirror they've ever known—their life before graduation—is taken away and replaced with one that distorts them in a different way? It's no wonder they're searching for an identity.

The journey toward embracing an identity in Christ isn't easy, nor is it easy to guide others through it. We all struggle daily to embrace an accurate view of ourselves, fighting off the messages that constantly distort who we are. College-age people need leaders to hold up the mirror of Scripture, of God's love and grace, to give them an accurate picture of who they are. May you be faithful in guiding people to their true image, that of Christ.

CHAPTER 4

THE SEARCH FOR MEANING

Recently I was catching up with Shane, one of my students. He's a sophomore at a university about an hour away, so I hadn't seen him in a while. So when I saw him after church one Sunday, I was eager to check in. "How's life?" I asked him.

Now, my students know me well enough to recognize that when I ask them this question, I want an honest answer. So Shane said, "You really want to know?"

I looked at him and said, "I wouldn't have asked if I didn't."

He replied, "Are you sure you have time?"

With that comment, I knew Shane had a lot on his mind.

We found a place to talk, and Shane started telling me about all the things he'd been thinking about: Life, work, relationships, identity—all the great post-high school stuff. And I have to admit, I love these conversations. The thought processes of college-age people are so interesting to hear. They think through every angle of a situation and ask a thousand questions of themselves. But because they lack life experience, their thoughts and questions often turn into confusion. And to be honest, it's kind of fun watching a person squirm, listening to them make something simple much more complex than it actually is. It's not the confusion I enjoy; it's being a part of their road to clarity. It's a wonderful moment when I see a person realize what he wants in life or figure out the answer to a question he's been wrestling with for months.

Anyway, Shane told me about the pressure he felt to pick a career path. He'd declared a major, but in his mind he still had two more years to make a firm decision. Shane explained that his dad wanted to make sure that Shane would be able to support himself and a family one day. So Shane's dad was starting to put more and more pressure on Shane to buckle down and focus on his future. This urging might sound reasonable to an adult, but not necessarily to a college-age person for whom choosing a career translates into choosing an identity. And as we've seen, they simply aren't ready to make that decision yet. College-age people resist the pressure to choose a vocation because they want their lives to be defined by something more than what they do or what they own. They want their lives to have meaning.

Shane is a very sharp guy. He knew he'd have to make some decisions about his future, but he wasn't as concerned about it as his parents were. For him, future responsibilities were just that— the future. He was more concerned about his life right then. He was consumed with sorting out who he was and what he wanted out of life. And he believed that if he could get that part figured out, the career piece would take care of itself. For his parents, finding a career was meaningful in and of itself. For him, determining what he wanted was the door to meaning.

Shane was asking the same questions most college-age people ask, questions for which they have no real answers: Should he continue in school and pursue a master's degree right away? Could he afford more school? Should he work for a few years after graduation and then go to grad school? Did he need grad school at all? Those of us who've been where Shane is know these questions have no right or wrong answers. But college-age people need to ask them just the same. They're a crucial part of the search for meaning. And that search is tightly tied in to the search for identity.

THE WONDER YEARS

The search for meaning during the college-age years can be exhilarating. The whole world is open to them. They're not tied down by anything. They're free to move in any direction. They're filled with the hope of a future that will be the realization of all their dreams. The hope of having a meaningful future is effortless. But discovering meaning for today is another story.

This struggle for a sense of meaning is bumpy, messy, often frustrating, and lonely. And because college-age people are under so much pressure to make some kind of plan for the future, they often jump through this stage too quickly in an effort to find something—anything—in which they can find meaning. Sometimes they land on faith and find real meaning and purpose. But most often, I find, college-age people get a temporal sense of meaning from at least one of three areas: Vocation, school, and relationships.

None of these areas is a problematic place to find *some* sense of meaning or purpose. But college-age people have a tendency to stop here, to vest themselves fully in what they do or whom they know. Finding meaning to the point of embracing these parts of life as their identity can be detrimental to their faith. When we understand the pull of these areas—and know how to guide college-age people on to deeper meaning in an identity through Christ—we can save them tremendous heartache.

Vocation

Every job can offer some sense of identity, but the ones that become the most tempting rest stops on the way to finding meaning are careers valued by the culture. Those who are lucky enough to find a good-paying job right out of college can put a halt to their search for meaning because it feels as though they've already found it. Those who don't find those jobs can feel like they're in a holding pattern—stuck without a purpose until the "right" career comes along.

My friend Suzy is a great example of someone who—without knowing it—had equated meaning and purpose with vocation. She'd graduated from college but was working part-time, not knowing what kind of work she wanted to do. We were talking one afternoon when she said in obvious frustration, "Chuck, I'm 25, and at some point I have to decide what I'm going to do with my life!" For Suzy, there was no direction, no meaning, without some kind of vocation.

The longer we talked, the clearer it was to me that Suzy had never planned on being defined by her work. But in the years since high school, most of her friends had either gotten married or were beginning their careers. From her perspective, their lives had meaning and purpose, and hers didn't. Suzy wasn't married and didn't have a boyfriend, so she felt like marriage and family were far off. She was out of college, so she'd lost the sense of purpose that comes from having a goal like graduation. So the only thing she could think of to give her an identity, to give her life meaning, was work. She didn't realize that a job could never quite provide the sense of *true* meaning and fulfillment she was hoping for.

Work is clearly a big stepping stone in the search for identity and meaning in this stage of life. College-age people explore all kinds of jobs and eventually figure out what they're good at, what they like to do, and what they don't like to do; it's part of the differentiation and integration process we discussed in chapter 2. From a spiritual standpoint, work often helps college-age people get an idea of the unique gifts and passions God has given them. Work can be a very important part of who they are and where they find meaning. But unless we ministry leaders help them make the connection between the work they do and their purpose as children of God, we'll leave them with a half-formed sense of meaning.

Perhaps the most essential connection we can help them make is that any kind of work can be kingdom work. I recently received the following email from a girl in our ministry.

> My name is Stacy, and I've been attending college group at Cornerstone for about five months now. It's absolutely amazing how much my life has changed in the few months I've been here. God has been doing some absolutely amazing things and put some things on my heart that I needed to talk to someone about. Originally, my plan was to transfer up to San Jose for anthropology to eventually get my doctorate in archeology, but lately I've just been realizing I'm not as passionate about that—and I feel I really want to spend my life doing something for God. I was thinking something along the lines of being a Christian counselor. I just need some guidance right now. If you have any ideas, that would be fantastic. I'm a little lost right now as to what I should be doing.

She had somehow gotten the idea that having a career in archeology couldn't possibly be "doing something for God." A lot of college-age people are like Stacy—well-intentioned young adults who find themselves torn between the work they're drawn to and the work they think God "wants" them to do. But God can and will use them no matter what kind of work they do. Just look at the wide array of people God uses in the Bible—everyone from a young shepherd (1 Samuel 17:12-50) to simple fishermen (Matthew 4:18-22) to a teenage girl (Luke 1:26-38).

We don't want our college-age people to fall into the trap of searching for meaning solely through their work. Jobs change, interests change, circumstances change. Lasting meaning comes when we know God is using our work to build the kingdom, and our role is to guide college-age people toward this conclusion.

School

Brett was a senior in high school when his mom died. After her funeral we talked for a while, and the subject of his future came up. I asked him what kind of plans he had after high school. He said, "I'm just going to see how it goes. I'm probably just going to take a few classes at the community college and then see what happens." At first, I thought his vague plans had to do with his mom's illness and death—I guessed he hadn't had much time to think about his future when his present situation was so difficult. But as we talked, it became clear that he'd been planning on community college long before his mom got sick. The fact was he just didn't know what he wanted to do, but figured he should at least keep going to school.

This attitude has become the norm for college-age people. Graduating from high school is no longer a step into adult life; it's simply the end of one kind of school and the start of another. College itself is less a move toward a particular career than a place to keep figuring out life. It's a time to experience different ways of life and discover what's out there, taking one step at a time.

College becomes the first step on the journey toward meaning, no matter what school the college-age person attends.

Most college freshmen have no clue what they want to do with their lives. Like Brett, they hope college will somehow give them the sense of direction they know they'll need eventually. Even high school graduates who don't go to college see these post-high school years as a time for searching, for exploring, for experimenting. They have little sense that they need to land anywhere anytime soon.

Every person's journey through the post-high school years is different, but those who go on to some kind of graduate school often find themselves clinging to their college experiences in an effort to give their lives meaning. Like work, school can provide an identity, one that carries with it a false sense of purpose.

Whether students get deeply involved in campus activities, discover their rebellious side, seek out academic success, or focus on preparing for a career by diving into a major, it's easy to use these niches as substitutes for real purpose. College tends to create its own micro-society, and when a student finally finds a place in that society, it feels wonderful and fulfilling. But in reality, finding meaning in the roles they play in college only prolongs the search for meaning. Once school is over, they begin the cycle of losing their sense of purpose and searching for meaning all over again.

We don't need to burst the bubbles of college students who've found a sense of purpose in their lives on campus. But just as we do when we're talking about vocation, we need to ask questions of these students and help them discover the ways the gifts and passions they're discovering at school might translate into the rest of their lives. We can ask them what they're learning about themselves and get them thinking about the ways God might use what they're discovering in other parts of their lives.

Relationships

The hope that intimate relationships—marriage in particular—will bring meaning and fulfillment is common among college-age people. Although vocation brings an initial sense of meaning and purpose, in the back of their minds, marriage is the icing on the cake for this age group. Women in particular are under tremendous cultural pressure to find their purpose in the context of marriage and motherhood.

Genesis 3 describes a characteristic of women that's very interesting to me. God says the woman's desire will be for her husband. In my marriage, I find that my wife is usually the one wanting us to spend more time together. Of course I love being with her, but she seems to have a stronger need for togetherness than I have. It might just be that I'm a great guy, an absolute hunk of a man with a magnetic personality (I'm sure I'll catch wind of someone who doesn't know I'm joking.) But I think the real reason is that women are wired to long for relationships in a way that men aren't. I find that the young women in my college ministry are far more likely to turn to their relationships for a sense of meaning than the young men are.[10] I'm not saying men don't find meaning in relationships as well, but the temptation to let relationships become the *only* source of meaning seems to hit women in a unique way.

God designed us for intimacy, but we're designed to find our true identity and meaning in our relationship with God—even when we experience intimacy with him through other people. I've found that college-age people need our help to see when they're putting too much stock in a relationship. Here again, asking questions is the best way to get young adults thinking through the decisions they're making and looking at the deeper issues

---

10 I recommend a resource titled, "What Makes a Woman Beautiful," which is a free download on www.collegeleader.org.

involved. You can ask questions such as, "How does this relationship help you grow in your faith and connection with God?" or "How do you think you'd feel if this relationship didn't work out?" or "How do you feel when you're not with this person?" or even "What older couples do you admire because of their relationship with each other? What do you think makes those relationships work?" Questions like these help college-age people connect the dots a bit more, giving them a clearer picture of how their relationships are affecting them.

DANGEROUS MINDS

College-age people don't know what direction they'll go until they know what they want from life. This hurdle—and it's a big one—keeps them from thinking practically. We need to understand that they're still highly idealistic about the wide-open future. This time can be very frustrating and confusing for college-age people, but it's also a wonderful period of exploration and imagination. We do them a great disservice if we try to rush them through it. Instead, our role as leaders is—once again—to guide them through this idealistic stage with grace, patience, and wisdom.

Having this knowledge about the search for identity, we recognize that college-age people need to know more about who they are before they can figure out where they'll find meaning in their lives. Developmentally, this focus on who they are and what they want is normal and even necessary for college-age people. But from a theological perspective, the near-constant emphasis on personal fulfillment holds some real dangers.

The search for meaning is a dynamic process for everyone, no matter the age. But the people and things we look to in an effort to determine meaning—work, school, relationships—quickly become the centering, unifying hinges that hold our ideas about meaning together. The hope and trust we place in them will not only drive our pursuits, but will ultimately cause those hinges to function as "God" in our lives.

For late adolescents, the hinge is often their own desire. They depend on their feelings to show them what's meaningful. Therefore, "God" for most college-age people is whatever they desire most at any given moment. The danger, obviously, is that this is a faulty god, one that turns them into egocentric idolaters. I know that sounds harsh, but college-age people need us to be frank with them, to point out the logical implications of the way they think and believe. Then they need us to show them a more biblical perspective on meaning.

We can help them in a few different ways. First, because they so easily find meaning in the here and now, we have to expose them to what is *eternally* meaningful. Exposure to things such as serving their communities, caring for the poor and oppressed, and discovering all the ways God is working in other parts of the world can really help shape their definitions of meaning. We need to draw them to the Bible, to prayer, to a life of ministry, to relationships formed through Christian fellowship. And we need to tell them stories of our own struggles to find meaning.

Secondly, we keep asking questions. I find that generalities get me nowhere. College-age people are ready for straightforward, even pointed questions that push back on their assumptions about themselves and their lives. Here are four questions I find particularly helpful.

1. **What do you want?** College-age people often answer this question with, "I'm not sure." It's not that they haven't thought about it; they just don't know the answer yet. So we need to keep digging. Eventually, college-age people get to the point where

they can articulate the desire to find meaning in something lasting, something eternal. They know jobs and school and relationships aren't enough. They end up placing their meaning in those areas because it feels good to find an answer to the question of what they want. But when we push them a bit, they do want to find God's purpose and have meaning come from living the lives for which God created them.

Once they get to the point of acknowledging that they want what God wants, we need to stay connected and continue asking questions about how they might figure out what that is. What might that purpose look like? Having someone walk them through this exploration is vital. You can be the person who keeps them engaged with the Christian community and keeps encouraging them to continue moving forward in that search.

2. **What do others want for you?** Asking this question will give you an idea of the pressures your college-age people are facing from others. These expectations are more burdensome to them than they'll let on most of the time. Your conversations can provide a huge sense of relief as you help them process what kind of obligations they have to other people. If they constantly give in to what others think they should be doing without figuring out what God is calling them to, they'll never find that deeper sense of purpose. Rather, they will, again, end with a substituted identity in what others want for them.

Ultimately, it doesn't entirely matter what others want for them. Our goal is to help them see what *God* desires for them and to help them embrace it. Our goal is for them to want to align their desires with God's alone. Of course, the bigger challenge here is to help them discern what God *does* desire for them. Answering this question begins with an understanding of the God of the Bible and a sense of who God made them to be. It's virtually impossible to help people determine God's plans for their lives if they don't have some degree of self-awareness. God has uniquely gifted each person (Ephesians 4:11-16, Romans 12:3-8) to live and function in society differently. Of course, a general calling is on all of us to follow God's will and commands in our lives, but ultimately, answering the question of what God desires of us goes back to each person's unique identity.

3. Why? It doesn't matter what question you asked or what answer they gave. Asking this question is a great way of keeping conversations going and helping college-age people move past surface answers. Their lack of life experience limits the depth with which they can explore some concepts on their own. So if, for instance, one of your young women tells you she really wants a boyfriend, asking "why" can help her think through her motivations. She might be lonely, she might think she needs to find a guy before she gets out of college, she might be ready to share her life with someone. Whatever her reasons, it's likely she hasn't put much thought into them. She just knows what she wants. The "why" question helps college-age people get a closer look at their own hearts. As they respond, pay attention and point them to the ways their faith can help them deal with the fears or loneliness or pressure they're facing.

4. Where do you find meaning today? College-age people are constantly looking to the future for meaning, but what about today? What is meaningful to them *now?* Their responses, again, will give you a glimpse into their priorities. Discussing this question also helps you connect with them on a less intense level. Find out what's meaningful in their lives and make an effort to ask them about it from time to time. When they know you care, they'll take your more challenging questions and insights more seriously.

That idea brings me to my third suggestion for helping college-age people find meaning and purpose in God: Tell them what you're doing. There's no reason to hide your role in their lives or pretend you're just their pal. Let them know you see yourself as a helpful guide through what can be an incredibly difficult journey. Tell them this role is meaningful to you and you believe it's what God desires of you (2 Timothy 2:2, Titus 2). They don't need more friends (well, some of them do). They need someone who will be honest with them, who will push them, who will invest the time and effort it takes to help them work through the process of building a life of purpose.

CHAPTER 5

DESPERATELY SEEKING INTIMACY

I was intimate with my wife last night, and it was one of the greatest nights we've ever had together. Simply amazing.

Is that kind of weird for me to say? A little too much information for you? Don't need to know about my sex life? Well, you're right. You don't. But sex isn't the only kind of intimacy I have with my wife. In fact, some of the most intimate times I've shared with her had nothing to do with sex. We've had moments of true, heart-to-heart connection that didn't involve any physical contact at all. We've had arguments that have hit both of us at the core, creating levels of intimacy I never knew existed. Intimacy can be created in all kinds of encounters, not just sexual ones.

Intimacy is knowing a person deeply and allowing that person to know you in the same way. It's the ability to be close, loving, and honest with another person. And it develops through time, communication, trust, and vulnerability.

Looking at these descriptors, it's clear what kinds of skills need to be in place in order for a person to build true, healthy intimacy with others. For example, because intimacy involves getting to know other people and allowing them to get to know you, it requires both people to know themselves. In other words, intimacy demands a certain level of identity development so we can disclose who we are to another person. Having a sense of who we are and being able to articulate that identity to someone is a prerequisite for an intimate relationship.

If that sense of identity is underdeveloped, intimate relationships have the potential to do tremendous damage to the people involved. We all know young people who've gotten involved in relationships in which they jettison all of their values and replace them with the values of the other person—a classic image of the Substitute stage of development. The person with the stronger sense of identity can dominate the relationship, putting an end to any kind of true intimacy for either of them.

Robert and Emily began dating on one of our winter retreats. They met each other on a chairlift and hit it off immediately. But Robert was settled into a career path, and Emily found herself floating through life with no real direction. Robert had experienced enough to know what he was good at, what he wanted to do, and most importantly, who he was in Christ. Emily, however, was in a very different place. She didn't have any real sense of who she was or what direction she wanted her life to go. Consequently, their relationship lacked intimacy. At one point Robert told me about how much he cared for Emily, but he said he realized she just wasn't ready for a relationship with any amount of depth. The relationship was stunted because of her lack of self-awareness. Like many college-age people, Emily couldn't be intimate with Robert because she lacked the ability to disclose herself.

At the same time, college-age people long for intimacy. You could see it in Robert and Emily's relationship. At this age, they begin to outgrow friendships based mostly on shared location. They begin to sift out those friends who were little more than acquaintances and look for more meaningful relationships—both platonic and romantic. Anyone working with college-age people must understand this longing for intimacy and how we can help guide them toward biblically mature conclusions about how to develop true connections with others and, most importantly with God.

As I said, there's more than one kind of intimacy. In fact, there are four kinds of intimacy. Sometimes a relationship will involve all four kinds, sometimes only one or two. But each kind of intimacy meets a specific type of need for belonging that exists in each of us.

1. Spiritual. This type of intimacy is often the easiest to find because we tend to gather with those who share our spiritual beliefs. Despite a variety of differences in personality, an immediate level of intimacy happens when we discover someone shares our brand of spirituality. College-age people often initiate relationships based on this one aspect of intimacy, making it a kind of "front door" to lifelong relationships.

2. Intellectual. This kind of intimacy suggests that two people have common interests in fields such as culture, politics, hobbies, morality, and ethics. Like spiritual intimacy, intellectual intimacy often leads to quick connections. A simple conversation can initiate an immediate level of intimacy.

3. Physical. We're probably most familiar with this kind of intimacy. Physical intimacy speaks of anything physically oriented: Touching, hand holding, hugging, sexual activity, snuggling. It implies that we've made a mutual agreement with someone else about sharing personal space—we're allowing and even welcoming another person to be physically close to us. That agreement alone can be a sign that other kinds of intimacy are present in the relationship.

4. Emotional. This type of intimacy is a little more complex and much more subjective than physical intimacy. For a relationship to have emotional intimacy, both people have to be willing to disclose their thoughts, feelings, and beliefs. But the thoughts and feelings and beliefs that create intimacy come from a person's sense of themselves. In order for emotional intimacy to occur, each person needs to have developed a certain amount of personal identity. Emotional intimacy also requires trust, which takes time and a willingness to be vulnerable with others.

Each type of intimacy calls for a level of maturity that few college-age people have reached. But the desire for intimacy is present just the same. This combination of factors is why they need guidance as they pursue intimacy in all its forms. They need caring leaders who can help them figure out what might be keeping them from forming healthy, intimate relationships. They need us to help them recognize the limits of late-adolescent intimacy. And they need us to help them connect the dots between their longing for human intimacy and their longing for intimacy with God.

THE PURSUIT OF INTIMACY

Naturally, college-age people are able to have intimate relationships well before they have a fully formed sense of identity; the pursuit of intimate relationships can actually be a huge part of their identity development. The closer they connect with other people, the better the process of differentiation and integration will be. The lack of deep interaction with others can have a detrimental impact on identity formation. The ability to disclose oneself and have others reciprocate is a big part of moving from one developmental stage to the next. At the same time, we need to understand how a lack of maturity and clear sense of identity can turn intimate relationships into inhibiting relationships.

In many ways, late-adolescent relationships aren't that different from mid-adolescent relationships. In mid-adolescence (ages 14 to 17), relationships tend to be fairly shallow. The minimal abstract-thinking capacity and egocentric perspective of mid-adolescents limit deeper levels of intimacy. Because they aren't able to see the intimate parts of their own hearts, they aren't able to disclose those parts to others.

Of course, they can share to some degree—and some are more capable than others—but there are definitely limitations. No matter how much two 15-year-olds know about each other, they're biologically limited in their ability to understand others at a deeper level. Relationships in this stage of life are far more strategic than intimate. In other words, mid-adolescents form relationships based on what they can get out of it, rather than what they can give to someone else.

The egocentric outlook of mid-adolescents leads them to push for dominance in their relationships in an effort to fulfill their personal agendas. This push is fairly unconscious—it's more developmental than devious. But think, for example, about the reasons high school students date. For most mid-adolescent guys, dating is centered on sexuality. Their hormones are running rampant, and when they think about relationships, those thoughts are primarily centered on sexual encounters and fulfilling those desires in some way. Girls, on the other hand, are driven toward dating relationships by a different egocentric desire: Status. Most high school girls date for the prestige it brings. Having a boyfriend— especially one who can boost their self-esteem in some way—can be a major motivator for dating. These adolescent tendencies are what drive the pursuit of intimacy in the high school years.

This selfish approach to relationships certainly isn't limited to mid-adolescence, but the typical teenager does eventually develop the ability to focus on others. Sex remains a motivator for a lot of college-age guys; but for most, the pursuit of intimacy moves beyond *just* sexual encounters. And college-age women can still be motivated by status. But in both their dating relationships and peer friendships, their pursuit of intimacy also moves beyond that single-minded mid-adolescent approach.

For both men and women, their quest for identity motivates their pursuit of intimacy in the college-age years. They're looking for affirmation on who they're becoming. They're looking for connections with people like them so they can continue to move through the differentiation and integration process. And, because they no longer have the same kind of intimate relationship with their parents that they once had, college-age people are in search of new "families"—or new relationships with their actual families—in which they can find a sense of belonging.

Lance—a guy in my college group—is a perfect example of these changing motivations. I was working in my office one afternoon when Lance stopped by to say hi—at least that's why he *said* he'd stopped by. I was on the phone when Lance poked his head in the door and said, "What's up?" I gave him the finger—the pointer finger—to let him know I'd be a minute and motioned for him to sit down. Once I got off the phone I said, "Hey, man, what are you up to?"

"Oh, not much," he said.

He had a blank look on his face, so I responded, "What do you mean, 'Not much'? It seems like something's on your mind."

"No, not really. I had to drop off some stuff for our Mexico trip. Since I was in the area, I thought I'd stop by and say hi."

"Well, hi." I just stared back at him. You see, I know him pretty well. I could tell by the way he fidgeted in the chair and looked around the room that something was on his mind. So I just stared at him with a smile on my face, saying nothing.

"Okay! I was wondering if you had a few minutes to hang out." He caved, we laughed, and we went to grab a bite to eat.

Lance is a 20-year-old guy who's thinking through all his relationships, particularly his relationship with his parents. He wanted to feel closer to them, but some hurdles were in the way. The biggest one was that he'd spent his high school years trying to separate from his family, which is normal; but a few years later, he found himself feeling like he couldn't talk to them. He longed for intimacy, but he had no idea how to move toward it.

He boldly declared that he really wished he could talk to his parents, but he didn't know where to start. In his words, he was "constipated" when it came to figuring out relationships. He longed for a deeper connection with people now that he was thinking through so many aspects of life, but he was stuck.

After high school, when friends have scattered and family relationships have changed, college-age people find themselves without intimate relationships—often for the first time. The feelings of isolation and detachment that follow can serve as a catalyst into a deeper search for intimacy.

DEVELOPING INTIMACY

The challenge for college-age people comes in learning how to find and nurture the kind of intimate relationships they crave. As leaders, we can help them identify the ways they might be unintentionally sabotaging intimacy and guide them in the process of developing the maturity and skills they need to create intimacy.

I find that most college-age people run into five specific challenges when trying to develop intimate relationships.

1. Lack of boundaries. Without going into a whole explanation, let me use the most obvious example of confusion over boundaries. Sarah and Matt have been friends for a few months. They eat most of their meals together at the student union; they study together. They go to movies and concerts and coffee shops together. They can talk for hours about anything and everything. Sarah thinks they're moving toward dating, but Matt has no intention of dating Sarah. For him, this relationship is just a really great friendship.

College-age women like Sarah often get confused and get hurt when they realize the guy isn't actually interested in a dating relationship. They can't understand how a guy can be so emotionally and intellectually intimate without wanting to take the relationship deeper. But men like Matt end up just as confused. They don't know what they did wrong. They tried to be a "good friend" and had no idea their female friends had other expectations.

You undoubtedly know lots of Sarahs and lots of Matts. The issue that comes up is primarily one of boundaries. Both parties lack the maturity to know how to draw appropriate lines around what a relationship is and what it isn't.

2. Lack of self-knowledge. Intimacy also comes to a halt because few college-age people know themselves as well as they think they do. Between the ages of 18 and 25, the human brain goes through massive amounts of change. It's like a bookend to puberty but without the crazy hormone shifts. Still, these changes make for a great deal of inconsistency in young adults. They're constantly processing new ideas and experiences, which means their opinions and beliefs change almost hourly. Consequently, they often contradict themselves on a regular basis. This inconsistency impedes the pursuit of intimacy. College-age people aren't able to offer a true and trustworthy "self" to a relationship because they haven't found that "self" yet. The constant change and unpredictability can create frustration and tension in relationships, which makes intimacy hard to come by.

3. Lack of trust. Intimacy requires honest communication and vulnerability. But for college-age people, trust in others' honesty and motives can be difficult to find. They're beginning to realize most of their high school relationships were strategic and manipulative in some way. And, because of their stronger abstract-thinking capabilities, they also realize they may have been the victim of someone else's manipulation! Once they've come to this point, they become wary of letting themselves be vulnerable with others. And if they can't trust someone, they can't build intimacy.

4. Lack of disclosure. This rude awakening to the manipulative power of relationships has another ripple effect that inhibits intimacy. College-age people are able to pick and choose what they reveal about themselves—and what they hold back. They might reveal part of themselves in one relationship and a different part of themselves in another. This behavior is fairly normal and in some ways helps college-age people with the differentiation and integration process. But it also has two very unhealthy results.

The first issue is that this tendency to disclose only part of themselves in any one relationship gives college-age people the illusion of intimate relationships. Because they think they have deep connections already, they never learn how to wholly reveal themselves to another person. And without learning how to completely disclose themselves, they risk never experiencing real intimacy.

The second problem is that this lack of disclosure cheats the person's friends out of the intimacy *they* want in the relationship. They think they're getting something they're not—a true, honest friendship. Whether they're on the giving end or the receiving end of the incomplete disclosure, college-age people find themselves unknowingly accepting a poor substitute for real intimacy.

5. Fear of betrayal. This issue is less an "age stage" problem than a "human condition" problem. College-age people have lived long enough to have been hurt by someone. Whether it was a dating relationship that ended badly, a friendship that fell apart, or their relationship with their parents being shattered in some way, the heartbreak that comes with having been betrayed lasts a very long time. That pain creates fear, and that fear creates a huge barrier to intimacy.

The desire for intimacy among college-age people drives them to make all kinds of decisions and changes. If left on their own, without Christian mentors to help them navigate the tumultuous waters of relationships, they will definitely capsize.

WHAT THIS ISSUE MEANS FOR YOUR MINISTRY

As we take on the discipleship of college-age people, it's important for us to understand their quest for intimacy. I've talked about the challenges this quest presents as late adolescents become more aware of who they are and how they connect with others. As these young people build relationships, they're using what they learn about themselves and others to hone in on their sense of identity. They manage the speed bumps that hinder intimacy— their immaturity, their fears, their still-developing understanding of themselves—and do their best to reconnect with their families and connect for the first time with the wide array of friends they meet in this new stage of life.

As we watch the college-age people we know struggle with intimacy, we can help them ask new questions of themselves and of God. But we have to know how to recognize what their struggles mean. Here are some connections I've seen between the intimacy issues college-age people face and the deeper, spiritual issues we need to tap into.

- They might have heard their youth leaders or pastors talk about having an intimate relationship with God, but they haven't been able to fully understand what that means until now. This age stage is the perfect time to ask questions about how they can develop their relationships with God.

- The struggle to fully disclose themselves to others can point to a college-age person's struggle to be fully real with God, to fully trust God, and to feel fully accepted by God.

- If they spent their high school years strategically pursuing relationships for their own benefit, then it's likely they have a similar relationship with God.

- Because their thoughts and feelings are constantly changing, we can assume their thoughts and beliefs about God are also coming into question and changing.

- The ability to create the illusion of intimacy with others often means a college-age person knows how to do the same with God.

The pursuit of intimacy has much larger implications in the discipleship process of college-age people than we might think. It goes much deeper than a desire for friendship and a longing to overcome feelings of isolation or detachment. It's a quest for connection, for community, for the kind of fellowship that I believe is one of the hallmarks of the Christian faith.

To give college-age people the guidance they need as they pursue intimacy with others and with God, we need to make sure we're giving them clear messages about who God is, about who we are, and about who God created them to be. Here are five ideas for communicating these messages.

1. Talk about the nature of God. We can't assume college-age people know who God is, even if they grew up in the church. We certainly can't assume they're moving toward a deeper knowledge of God during these years. For many college-age people, the opposite is true. But they're at the perfect stage for discovering God in new ways. And encountering God is essential as they work through the identity-formation process and seek out intimate relationships. In the midst of the constant changes in their lives, they need to see God's dependability, consistency, and trustworthiness (Psalm 9:10, 33:4; Hebrews 13:8). And they need to see God as the most important influence in their identity formation—someone with characteristics that are definitely worth integrating.

2. Encourage intimacy with God. We are designed for intimacy—and that intimacy begins with God (Matthew 22:37-38). We need to remind college-age people that their longing for intimacy is one of the ways they're growing closer to God. God is actively revealing himself to us through Scripture, through the Holy Spirit, through our spiritual leaders, through nature and friendships, and so on. But in order for true intimacy to occur in that relationship, we also have to be willing to personally reveal ourselves to God. College-age people who've grown up in the church have learned how to go through the motions of faith but still hold their hearts back from God (Isaiah 29:13, Matthew 15:8). We need to both model and encourage real, honest relationships with God. The same trust, vulnerability, and communication that build intimacy in human relationships can help college-age people let down their guard and let God into their lives. Encourage them to develop a meaningful prayer life and to surround themselves with people who draw them closer to God.

3. Model vulnerability. College-age people are genuinely interested in who we are, and we need to embrace this curiosity as an open door for discipleship. The more we initiate emotional,

DESPERATELY SEEKING INTIMACY

spiritual, and intellectual intimacy, the more they'll reciprocate. Remember, they desire it but rarely know how to pursue it. We need to show them.

4. Be consistent. Developing any intimate relationship takes time and consistency, but this fact is especially true with college-age people. Their lives are filled with inconsistency, something that hinders intimate relationships. Consistency builds trust. It builds connections. It builds real friendships.

5. Ask questions. For new ideas, behaviors, and identity issues to stick, college-age people have to come to them on their own. Asking questions is the best way to help them think through the issues they face. Sometimes the simplest questions have the most impact: Why do you want to be close to other people? What interests you about other people? What do you think intimacy looks like? What do you think needs to be present in a relationship for there to be real intimacy? Do you think you're doing anything that could hinder intimacy with other people? Questions like these, asked in the context of a trusted mentorship, can help college-age people process their experiences with intimacy much more effectively.

Walking with college-age people takes a tremendous amount of time and intentionality on the part of leaders. But I hope you're beginning to see the important role you play in the life of a college-age person. They need us as leaders, but also as mentors and friends, as people they can count on to care for them during the upheaval of the post-high school years. They don't need big events or special programs to feel connected to the church. They need friendships with people who love them, are truly intimate with God, and understand the unique challenges they face in that pursuit.

CHAPTER 6

THE PURSUIT OF PLEASURE

Steve was a student in my ministry who, well, let's just say he really tested my patience. He was one of those people you spend a ton of time with, invest yourself in completely, and see… nothing. No change. Zip. Sometimes I felt like I was talking to a brick wall. He just never seemed to get what I was saying. He would nod, agree, talk about how he needed to change, and then walk away and continue living the exact same way as before. This pattern went on week after week, month after month—shoot, year after year!

Steve lived in the moment, moving from one social activity to the next, doing whatever he pleased, whenever he pleased, with little concern for any responsibilities he had. His self-proclaimed philosophy to life was to only do what *needed* (he would always emphasize this word) to be done in order to do what he wanted to do.

Don't get me wrong—he was a great guy to be around. He was extremely likable and very funny. He had lots of friends and made every event he attended more fun. But even his friends considered him flaky. He constantly failed to follow through with commitments he'd made.

At one point, Steve was desperate for a job, so one of his buddies set up an interview for him at the company where he worked. The interview was scheduled at 11:00 on a Tuesday morning. I remember that detail because Steve and I had planned on meeting for coffee later that same day. We'd been talking for quite some time about his getting a job and working toward supporting himself. So I was looking forward to hearing how the interview went.

Knowing Steve was usually late, I'd brought a book with me to the coffee shop. About 20 minutes after our scheduled meeting time, I saw Steve pull into the parking lot. I realized how excited I was for him. This job seemed like a great fit for him, and I was really hoping it would be a good step toward maturity for Steve. As soon as we sat down, I asked him about the interview. With no hesitation at all, he said, "Oh, I decided not to go."

"Why did you make that decision?" I asked him, trying very hard to keep the frustration out of my voice. He explained that he'd gotten a phone call from a friend the night before. Apparently, the friend needed to talk, and Steve said he felt like "God really wanted" him to be there for his friend.

"Wasn't the interview today?" I asked.

"Yeah, but we talked until, like, 4:30 in the morning," Steve replied. "He's having some major problems with his dad and is trying to figure out what he should do. So I just felt like God really wanted me to minister to him."

As the conversation went on, Steve explained that his friend had called him around 7, so they grabbed some dinner, watched a movie, and hung out for nine hours. When I asked him if he'd at least called to cancel the interview, he said, "I was planning on doing that tomorrow. I was just so tired after talking all night. I slept until 1:00 today." Then he threw in the real kicker. He said, "I figured if I woke up before 11:00, then I was supposed to go to the interview. If I didn't, then I just figured God didn't want me to have the job. I mean, God could've totally woke me up, right?"

That's when I changed the subject.

Not only did Steve blow a great opportunity, but he also showed no concern for the friend who'd stuck his neck out for Steve. And then he had the gall to blame God for his lack of follow-through and responsibility. If I'd have thought it would make a difference, I might have pressed Steve on these points. But we'd had enough similar conversations that I knew he just wasn't ready to make a change. He wasn't ready to give up self-centeredness for responsibility and self-control.

Not every college-age person is as irresponsible as Steve. But many college-age people struggle with self-discipline. Social pursuits take precedence over responsibilities. Seeking pleasure takes precedence over keeping commitments. Some young adults realize this attitude is problematic and wish they could be more disciplined. Others—like Steve—have found ways to rationalize their behavior, whether spiritualizing it, passing the blame to friends, or assuming they get a free pass on responsibility because they're young or popular or wealthy or smart, or whatever else they think will help them avoid being disciplined.

This area of college-age ministry might be one of the most difficult—not for the college-age people themselves, but for us as leaders. We—at least I—can get so frustrated, so fed up with the lack of self-discipline, the flakiness, the inconsistency, that it becomes hard to find the patience and understanding our college-age people desperately need from us. It's an area in which *we* must personally exercise self-control and commitment.

When I'm struggling to deal with people like Steve, I find it helpful to step back and think about why college-age people act this way. I know they aren't trying to be irresponsible—many of them really do want more maturity in this area. The fact is, a number of issues are going on in their lives that contribute to their strong need to seek out pleasure instead of reliability.

NEWFOUND FREEDOM

Trevor is a 23-year-old living in Southern California. He's finished a couple years' worth of college courses, works about 30 hours a week, and surfs every day. He saves money all year so he can spend his winter weekends snowboarding with his friends. He understands that one day he'll need to adjust his lifestyle; but for the time being, he's enjoying his freedom. His parents have given up trying to get him to make decisions about his future. He's told them plenty of times to back off, that he isn't going to change, and that he fully intends to enjoy his freedom while he has it.

Emily is 24 years old and living in downtown Chicago. She's completed a bachelor's degree in business and is working full-time in the shoe department at Nordstrom. She knows she could probably get a job that would be a first step toward a career, but this one provides flexibility and enough money for her to pay her rent and buy food and clothes. She never has to work before 10:00 in the morning, so she can stay out late with her friends. She doesn't want to get tied down to a job right now. She doesn't even know how long she'll stay in Chicago. But for now, she's enjoying her life.

Briana is a 19-year-old living in Portland, Oregon. She's taking classes at a community college and working full-time as a receptionist for a law firm. She lives at home with her parents, saving as much money as she can. She has a very strong desire to settle down and get married at some point, but those steps are definitely in the future. She's also been saving money so she can go to Europe for six months. Right now, her plans are to go back to school when she returns from Europe. But her parents want her to finish her education *before* she travels; they're concerned she won't want to go back after taking time off. Briana constantly tells her parents that school isn't going anywhere and that she wants to travel before she gets tied down to a job.

These stories are just three of the hundreds I could tell you about the value college-age people place on their newfound freedom. And you could undoubtedly tell plenty of your own. We all know college-age people who made smart decisions about how they'd use their increasing independence, people like Emily and Briana who take responsibility for themselves and their dreams and find ways to both explore their options and make some concrete plans for the future. And we all know people like Trevor who are so enamored with their freedom that they don't want to spend a second thinking about the responsibilities just around the corner.

Every college-age person deals with this new freedom differently. Some embrace it as a sign of adulthood and use it as an opportunity to prove themselves to their family and friends. Some have been somewhat independent for years—holding down jobs, buying their own cars, traveling on their own—and therefore take the freedoms that come after high school in stride. For the most part, however, I find that college-age people are so excited by their increased freedom that it takes a few years for them to even want to choose self-control over pleasure.

As leaders, we need to understand that it's natural—and necessary—for college-age people to explore their freedom. This journey is part of growing up, part of becoming an adult. And it's part of enjoying life. Trevor has a point—the "freedom" years are short, and we shouldn't deny our college-age people the chance to live life to the fullest and make memories that last forever (safely and legally, of course!). I also find that, for most of them, experience is a good teacher. College-age people learn pretty quickly that sleeping through class leads to low grades, staying up all night leads to poor job performance, and ignoring their homework doesn't fly with college professors. Before long, they'll find a bit more balance between freedom and responsibility. Our role isn't to force the process to go more quickly, but rather to guide them as they're learning the lessons themselves.

At the same time, helping them overcome that near-constant focus on themselves, on what feels good or fun or exciting, is our job as leaders. God calls us to a variety of decisions that aren't necessarily comfortable or desirable. In college-age ministry, we have to help people understand God's view of pleasure and discipline and the implications of both in their spiritual lives.

CHILDISH THINGS

I don't care if the people in my ministry have careers or if they're even pursuing them. I don't care if they're college graduates or high school dropouts. I don't care if they surf every day, live at home, and have their parents pay for everything. What I do care about is how these decisions impact their spiritual lives. Of course, we want to help them make good decisions about their futures, jobs and relationships. But what we really want is to point our people toward God. So rather than looking at the lack of discipline in a negative way, we can look at it as an open door for discipleship.

Let's go back to Steve—the guy I told you about at the beginning of the chapter. He lacks discipline in just about every area of his life. He lives completely in the moment. He has a terrible track record when it comes to following through with his commitments. And I fully believe he handles his faith the same way.

The way our college-age people live tells us a lot about where they're at spiritually. That statement is particularly true in the way they balance pleasure and self-control. They don't have much control over where they are in the search for identity or meaning—those developments come with time. But they do have control over how self-centered they are and how much weight they place on the pursuit of personal pleasure. They need us to call them to accountability and gently pull them out of their selfishness and into lives of deeper faith.

I love the insight 1 Thessalonians 1:3 gives us on this issue. Paul is writing to people in the Thessalonian church and says he remembers their "work produced by faith, [their] labor prompted by love, and [their] endurance inspired by hope in our Lord Jesus Christ." In the Greek language, the emphasis is clearly on the faith, love, and hope of Paul's audience. In fact, the way Paul structures his sentence stresses that these three qualities *produce* their work, labor, and endurance. His readers' spirituality was producing outward action, not vice versa. Outward actions are markers of spiritual condition. We can try to move people in a sociological or behavioral direction; but to be truly effective, we have to go much deeper. We must develop people's faith, love, and hope. And when we do, the outward actions take care of themselves (Matthew 23:25-26).

Very few college-age people know themselves well enough to recognize why they make the choices they make. They don't know how to think about their motives or the underlying beliefs influencing their behavior. They might say they love the Lord and desire to honor God with their lives, but they still live in the moment, think about their own needs and desires first, and lack a sense of responsibility and self-control. I believe they want to be faithful, that they want to make wise, godly choices that are expressions of their faith. They just need someone to help them see that faith demands discipline.

The apostle Paul offers three perspectives on discipline that I find especially useful for college-age ministry. Paul uses three different words for *discipline*, each one emphasizing a different aspect of the need for self-control in our lives: *Gymnazo, sophronismos,* and *taxis*. Talking our college-age people through Paul's perspective can give them insight into the ways discipline should play out in their lives.

The term *gymnazo* speaks of training for something with gymnastic-like discipline. It carries the sense of being focused on a very specific goal and working intensely toward that goal. We all know that gymnasts are well trained. They work for years, dedicating their entire lives to succeeding in their sport. Paul uses this term figuratively throughout the New Testament as a way of talking about the mental and spiritual training he believes Christians need to undergo. He uses this term in 1 Timothy 4:7-10, where he says,

> Have nothing to do with godless myths and old wives' tales; rather, train yourself to be godly. For physical training is of some value, but godliness has value for all things, holding promise for both the present life and the life to come. This is a trustworthy saying that deserves full acceptance. That is why we labor and strive, because we have put our hope in the living God, who is the Savior of all people, and especially · of those who believe.

The New International Version translates *gymnazo* as both *train* and *training* and specifically points this training in a spiritual direction. If the college-age people we're meeting with express a desire to be faithful and to live out their faith, they're going to need *gymnazo*. If they're not showing discipline in bodily form, they're most likely not doing much spiritual training either. If they're not disciplined, then they can't be godly. It's that simple. We have to help them understand that discipline in every area of life is training for true godliness.

At the same time, we need to be clear with them that the goal here isn't perfect behavior. Instead, their behavior points to what's going on in their spiritual lives. Their hearts are where our concern needs to be. College-age people can still get caught up in the idea that the appearance of a godly life is the end goal. (Look back at Steve's excuse for missing his job interview.) We need to tell them—sometimes over and over again—that we're concerned with what we see because it reflects their hearts. And their hearts are what we care about.

The second word Paul uses for discipline is *sophronismos*. This term speaks of having self-control along with sound judgment, and it's clearly an attribute God gives to believers. It speaks of an ability to make wise decisions and exercise self-control for the purpose of godliness. Paul uses this term in 2 Timothy 1:7, "For the Spirit God gave us does not make us timid, but gives us power, love and self-discipline."

Even when college-age people begin thinking about their identity, develop intimate relationships, and start searching for deeper meaning in life, they often lack the self-control to make their hopes become reality. Instead of going after a dream job that would require them to be at work by 8:00 in the morning, they'd rather continue to stay out late with their friends. Instead of saving money for grad school or mission trips, they run up debt on their credit cards. These judgment calls clearly aren't spiritually sound, but from the college-age, socially driven, and self-pleasing perspective, they make perfect sense.

We have to challenge college-age people to think about the judgment they use. More importantly, we have to help them understand that God has given them the ability to make sound decisions. They need to tap into that ability to start living faithfully.

The third word Paul uses is *taxis*, a military term that suggests structure, purposeful living, organization, and orderliness. Paul is thrilled with the *taxis* lifestyle he sees in the church at Colossae. He's encouraged that these believers have this kind of self-control. In Colossians 2:5 Paul writes, "For though I am absent from you in body, I am present with you in spirit and delight to see how disciplined you are and how firm your faith in Christ is." It's important to notice that Paul links their orderly lifestyle to their stable faith.

College-age people aren't typically characterized by the term *taxis*. But in order to stand firm in their faith, they need to develop this kind of discipline. Our role to help them think about how the lack of orderliness in their lives can negatively affect their faith.

Once again, we have to be careful that we don't encourage any kind of legalism in our college-age people. The kind of discipline Paul discusses here goes much deeper than regular quiet times, daily prayer, or a commitment to serve in the church. With this term, Paul urges Christians to develop a mindset in which we pursue something other than self-centered pleasure. We need to encourage Bible reading, time alone with God, prayer, and service as means toward an end. They are ways we build a godly life. They are not—in and of themselves—a godly life.

It's not that college-age people lack the desire to be godly. It's that they don't understand the role discipline plays in helping them grow into more mature Christians. For instance, college-age people are known for pointing to the search for "inner harmony" or "inner peace" as reasons they participate in religious services. While a tremendous amount of joy comes from worshiping God with our brothers and sisters in Christ, the point isn't to make ourselves feel better. Developing a sense of peace isn't the goal of godly living. The godly living comes first. Peace, harmony, spiritual well-being—these blessings are ways God honors personal godliness. The college-age focus on the self muddies this concept. So when we see our college-age people thinking about their faith in self-centered ways, we need to help them refocus.

MAKING THE CONNECTION

Replacing the pursuit of pleasure with self-control and discipline doesn't necessarily involve getting a solid job or putting aside trips to Europe. It involves pursuing godliness in every part of life. I find that most college-age people want to be more disciplined. They recognize it's the only way they can become the people they want to be. We can help them by asking questions about their decision-making processes, pointing them to Paul's words about discipline, and being solid examples of self-control. When we do, they'll ask more questions, think through the implications of their decisions, and begin integrating the characteristics of the godly people they see around them.

The pursuit of pleasure is really part of the pursuit of identity. For some, it's an aspect of the Explorer stage; for others, it's just another way to be a Floater with no direction at all. As I've said, we can help guide this process by consistently being there to help college-age people pursue godly discipline and faithfulness. We can't rush or force it, but we can certainly play a role in their identity transformation into faithful children of God.

CHAPTER 7

TRACKING DOWN TRUTH

Jimmy is one of the nicest guys you could ever meet. He's very outgoing, always has a smile on his face, and would do anything for anybody. He's a leader in every sense of the word. He serves in whatever ways are needed. He leads by example, reaches out to unpopular people, and has a tremendous heart for the helpless. He's a very confident yet humble guy who's a pleasure to have around. He's the kind of person you feel blessed to know.

One night after our college group wrapped up, Jimmy asked if he could meet with me sometime during the week. He said he'd been thinking about a few things for a long time and was wondering if we could talk through some of them. I told him I'd love to hang out with him, so we set up a time to have lunch.

A few days later, we met at Quiznos. We'd hardly sat down with our sandwiches when Jimmy's face turned bright red. He had a look of shame, regret, and confusion. He tried to say something, but his voice caught with emotion every time he started to speak. He seemed to be putting all his energy into keeping the tears from streaming down his face. His behavior was a bit surprising, so I pushed my food aside and said, "Hey, man, take your time. I've got all the time you need."

After a couple minutes, he was able to speak, his voice cracking with every word "I feel like I've done all the right things in my life. I've never walked away from the Lord and never even thought about it as an option. I've always tried to do what my parents and my pastors have told me…" And then he really broke down. He couldn't say another word as tears streamed down his face, and he looked away from me in shame. Not knowing what to say, I just waited silently.

After a minute or so, Jimmy lifted his head and looked right at me. His voice now steady, he said, "I'm so embarrassed, Chuck." He was looking at me as though he weren't sure he should keep talking. He wiped his eyes and nose and said, "Okay, I just have one question." He took a deep breath and said, "The question I have is, what does it mean to have faith?"

That was it. I have to tell you, I expected something much more dramatic and problematic. I quickly learned, however, that his uncertainty *was* dramatic and extremely problematic for him. The look of humiliation on his face was startling. He was so ashamed to ask that question. He assumed that with his background as a life-long Christian, he shouldn't have to ask. He thought someone with his leadership skills and responsibilities should know the answer. But I knew exactly what was happening to Jimmy, and—once I got over the shock of how normal his problem was—I knew why it was happening as well.

For the first time in his life, Jimmy was coming face to face with the reality that he didn't really have any faith of his own. He'd grown up in the church and knew what he was supposed to do and think, but he'd never really taken ownership of those beliefs. He knew how to give the answers his parents and pastors and youth leaders wanted to hear. He could regurgitate a lot of information. But he didn't have a clue *why* he was doing these things. He'd simply accepted what other people said, never thinking about it or questioning it. In recent months, he'd come to realize how shallow his faith really was. He knew that if he were ever going to have an authentic faith of his own, he needed to start over. His question to me was the first step in a journey toward a real, honest faith.

THE PURSUIT OF A PERSONAL WORLDVIEW

As we've seen, college-age people are thinking through all kinds of issues—identity, intimacy, the meaning of life, self-control. At the heart of all of these is the need to know what they believe and why they believe it. They can't find an identity or deep connection or a sense of purpose or motivation for self-control without evaluating and questioning their thoughts about God and faith.

No matter what kind of religious background college-age people come from—even if that background was a nonreligious one—during these years, they realize they've just accepted what was handed to them. For some of them, reaching that conclusion is no big deal. But most, like Jimmy, reach a point when they recognize the need to take a closer look at the beliefs with which they grew up and through which they've always seen the world. They realize they need to develop a worldview of their own.

Our purpose as leaders of college-age people is to help them create a biblically based, godly view of the world. Few enter their college-age years with a well-established worldview, but very few leave these years without one. Everything they're exposed to and taught influences their view of the world. Their cultural experiences, racial and social backgrounds, and families all shape their understanding of people, behavior, and God. And their worldview, in turn, shapes everything else

This worldview is up for grabs during the post-high school years because this period is often the first time young people experience worldviews that are different from their own. They meet people from other towns—possibly other countries—people with very different experiences and conclusions about life. As college-age people interact with new people and new ideas, they find that the assumptions they lived with for 18 years don't always hold up in this wider world.

It happens all the time—maybe it happened to you. When it does happen to our college-age people, it can be a make-or-break moment in their faith journey. Without a caring mentor to guide them through the process of worldview formation, college-age people too often abandon the faith altogether.

THREE DEAL BREAKERS

Earlier in the book, I talked about the way the college-age person's brain is changing. The most significant change is the shift from concrete thought to abstract thought. That shift has a tremendous impact on worldview formation. It's what causes a college-age person to ask questions she's never thought to ask before, to doubt what she once held as certain, and to have her understanding of truth get turned inside out.

The ability to think abstractly also causes college-age people to delve into areas of thought to which they never paid much attention before. I find that three such areas seem to cause the biggest problems for college-age people: Science, philosophy, and religion. It's not that these areas of thought are problematic on their own. It's that they encompass all of life's big questions: Who are we? Why are we here? Where did we come from? Where will we end up? What does it all mean? Every one of those questions lands a college-age person in one of these three areas of thought. Leaders need to have a solid grasp on the issues each area raises and the impact each area has on worldview formation.

1. **Science.** College-age people are often stunned to find that some people have radically different beliefs than they have. For the first time, they meet atheists, secular humanists, and agnostics who have well-crafted explanations for why they believe what they believe. These people might be a boss, roommate, professor, or girlfriend's brother. So often, college-age people will return from their first few months away from home with their heads full of new questions—and a lot of confusion.

These questions typically have some kind of foot in the science world. I don't mean they're necessarily "science questions," but questions about life and faith and God and meaning that have risen from conversations about anything from creation to human nature to politics. Those conversations often cause college-age people to see inconsistencies in the belief system with which they grew up. They sometimes point out faulty assumptions they've held for years. All of that rethinking can drastically shake the foundations of a college-age person's worldview.

For some, this disruption results in healthy introspection, the kind that eventually deepens and strengthens their belief system. But for others, this upheaval can be devastating. No matter how our college-age people handle the inevitable shake-up, we need to be prepared to guide them through the process of facing the tough questions of science.

We help them by acknowledging that conversations about faith and science aren't as black-and-white as they're often made out to be. The two aren't necessarily opposite sides of the same coin. In fact, I believe setting them up as such misses the whole point of faith.

For example, some groups put a great deal of effort into discounting the authenticity of the Bible using scientific evidence. At the same time, I'm well aware of the research that supports the historical veracity of the Bible, and I could argue with someone for days about why I believe science backs up the authenticity of Scripture. But I believed in the authority of the Bible long before I knew how to "prove" it, because faith, not scientific research, defines my belief in truth. My faith is an internal conviction that goes way deeper than other people's observations about creation.

Faith and science are two very different perspectives on how a person determines truth. It's a clash of worldviews. One relies on internal conviction and transformation to understand truth, the other on external data. It's futile to compare the outcomes of these two approaches to understanding truth. We want to focus on getting to the root of what determines the conclusions.

We also have to point out that science isn't flawless. Certain scientific theories that were once held as incontrovertible fact have now been proven false—the earth isn't flat, as science once proclaimed it to be. Most scientists acknowledge that much of what they believe is their best guess based on the evidence they have and that it very well could change if the evidence changes. The "facts" of science are still just human observations.

We also have to watch out for hypocrisy. Christians often rail against science when it seems to contradict what we believe, then embrace science when it supports us. But again, this response completely misses the point. Faith isn't based on what can be proven. It's based on our belief that God is who he says he is.

We want our college-age people to have the skills and confidence to navigate the sometimes-contentious world of science. But most of all, we want them to have a biblical worldview through which they can assess what they hear and learn without unnecessary confusion. Here's how we can help them get there:

- *Dismantle the common Western worldview that says science can explain everything.* We live in a culture that's been profoundly influenced—for good and not-so-good—by the Enlightenment. During that period, people began to consider science *the* instrument by which truth was determined. But this thinking flips faith upside down. It suggests that we should use science to determine the truths of our faith instead of using faith to determine the truths of science. Science is a means by which we can sometimes *find* something to be true, but it's not the deciding factor on what is, in fact, true. God alone determines truth (Psalm 111:7, 119:160; John 14:6).

- *Teach biblical theology.* College-age people are ready for a more intentional study of theology. Those who've grown up in the church most likely know a lot *about* their faith—the stories, the traditions, the basic tenets. But I find that very few college-age people know anything about why we hold to certain traditions or why those basic tenets are the ones to which we cling. They're ready for you to take them deeper into the theology behind their faith. So challenge them with your favorite texts, encourage them to ask hard questions of their faith and seek out answers, and give them permission to dig deeper and move beyond the "data" of their faith.

- *Explain the "faith" behind science.* Although few people will admit it, it takes just as much faith to accept science as fact as it takes to accept theology as fact; it's just faith in the people performing the research instead of faith in something else. We have faith that the scientists are giving us completely unbiased information, with no agenda, and for the sole benefit of uncovering truth. We have faith that there is such a thing as completely objective fact. I love the Discovery Channel as much as the next person, but that doesn't mean we should put science on a pedestal of truth.

- *Point out that all truth is God's truth.* If someone observing creation finds something to be "scientific truth," it's God's truth they've found. We need to reclaim truth as belonging to God, not science (1 Corinthians 3:18-23). The difference between a secular worldview and a Christian one is what, or Who, determines truth. Clarifying the role science plays in our lives is absolutely crucial to guiding college-age people toward spiritually mature conclusions about truth.

2. **Philosophy.** One of the most powerful influences on worldview development is philosophical discussion. With their expanding reasoning capabilities and desire to think through abstract issues at a much deeper level, college-age people are typically drawn to philosophical topics. Granted, some are less stimulated by intellectual conversation than others, but for the most part, college-age people are interested in talking about abstract issues like ethics and morality. And, like science, intellectual and philosophical thought can either affirm or oppose a young person's presuppositions about the world.

For many college-age people, these conversations first happen in a college classroom. Those who sit under a good philosophical teacher are often shocked at how deeply a person can think through a particular subject, how every question seems to be answered with another question. They hear ideas they've never heard before, discover perspectives on life, God, humanity, morality, and meaning they've never considered before. They feel their minds expanding and getting confused—and it's thrilling!

Even high school graduates who don't go to college will find themselves in conversations with coworkers, customers, landlords, roommates, and friends that will challenge their assumptions about ethical and moral issues. These conversations aren't limited to college classrooms. They come with the late-adolescent territory.

In my experience, the young people who best weather this enormous mental expansion are those with the theological chops to take in what they hear, look at it through the lens of what they believe, and come out with a far more thought-out faith than the one with which they began. But that good result calls for a good lens.

We can help our college-age people develop such a lens in these ways:

- *Don't dismiss philosophy.* Christians should never be mindless followers of faith. We need to know what we believe and why we believe it. We need to engage in the difficult conversations of life with thoughtfulness and intelligence. Philosophy isn't the enemy of faith. The enemy of faith is a reliance on human intelligence as the only source of knowledge. Too often, college-age people get dazzled by their own intellect, completely losing touch with a Christian perspective of life here on earth (Colossians 2:8).

- *Do some prep work.* Whenever possible, we need to prepare our college-age people for the philosophical issues that will come up in these years. As best we can, we need to engage their minds with the deeper conversations of faith—such as ethics and morality and meaning—so they're already considering what the Bible tells us about these issues and how that shapes belief. The goal isn't to keep them from asking questions, but to help them see that their faith offers answers to the deeper intellectual questions.

- *Properly define philosophy.* When college-age people encounter philosophical discussions for the first time, it can feel like they've uncovered the secret to an intelligent life. We need to point out that philosophy is simply one of the ways human beings try to make sense of the world. All people who engage in philosophical conversation and thought do so with a bias that's based in their worldview. We must focus on helping college-age people look past the conclusions that seem to make sense and into the presuppositions that brought about the conclusions. This simple understanding can prevent them from throwing away their faith just because someone makes what might seem like a logical argument against it (1 Corinthians 3:18-19). Philosophy, like science, doesn't have to conflict with faith.

- *Teach theology.* If we can help college-age people understand who God is, show them how to develop a deep and consistent faith, and teach them how to run everything through that lens, then we're headed in the right direction. We can't underestimate the importance of knowing God and looking at the world from a faith-based perspective (Colossians 1:9).

- *Point people toward Scripture all the time.* So many college-age people have never learned how to use their Bibles. Most think they know it well because they've heard Bible stories, done hours of devotions, filled out worksheets, and memorized verses. But just because they've completed those tasks doesn't mean they know how to read the Bible. It's our job to help them think through how well they actually know the Scriptures. Gaining knowledge and understanding from them will lead us to a proper understanding of truth and enable us to sort through arguments based on different worldviews.

3. Religion. When it comes to forming a worldview, no component is more important than religious belief. As I've already stated, theology ultimately drives every worldview, so religion is naturally going to play a huge role in worldview development. Along with science and philosophy, religion is very much on the radar of college-age people. They tend to be very "spiritual," but usually not in the biblical sense. For instance, they view personal faith as more important than being a part of a faith community.

Many college-age people attend organized religious gatherings on a fairly regular basis, but most seem to believe that no one religion holds the entire truth—they accept a kind of universalism in which each religion holds pieces of the truth, but none in its entirety. They rely on their own thoughts, feelings, and desires to sort out what's true and what isn't. Because they're engaging with spiritual issues, they believe they're being spiritual.

In many ways, this attitude is a reflection of the search for identity. College-age people long for community and seek justice for the helpless, but they're primarily concerned with their individual convictions. They'll accept or reject a religious community based on how if fits their desires, needs, and ideas, rather than letting the community inspire them to rethink the ideas they hold.

In this regard, churched and unchurched young people are very similar. Because college-age people are searching for an identity independent of their parents, the religious beliefs with which they grew up play a much less significant role than we might think. Most of us know people who grew up in the church and continue to embrace the faith with which they were raised. But on a national level, this group is so small that statisticians can't track them. The majority of college-age people embrace different beliefs than those of their parents—sometimes as a matter of principle, sometimes as an act of rebellion, but always as the result of their own convictions. This occurrence is not only true for Christians, but for every religious group. It's an age-stage issue, not a Christian one.

Religion plays a substantial role in the search for truth because all college-age people—whether consciously or not—are thinking through their theology. They typically consider their beliefs outside of any single religious system, investigating various beliefs and systems instead. As they explore, they need us to honor the process they're going through (with our understanding and openness to conversation), as well as give them the the tools they need to come to biblically mature conclusions. Here's how:

- *Know the basics.* The five major worldviews are naturalism, theism, pantheism, spiritualism/polytheism, and postmodernism. Each of the major world religions holds at least one of these worldviews. As leaders, we need to have at minimum a working understanding of each one if we're going to help people think through their beliefs.[11] We need to be prepared to talk about these worldviews with intelligence and engagement, but also with a solid understanding of Christian theology. When our college-age people come to us with difficult questions, we need to be ready to respond with understanding and conviction.

- *Hold firmly to our personal convictions.* When I say we need to have our theology in place, I don't mean we have to deny our own questions or doubts. In fact, our efforts to wrestle with the questions of faith can let our college-age people know that it's possible to be a person of faith and still reexamine your worldview now and then.

---

11 For more on helping our students think through their beliefs, see www.collegeleader.org/resources-links-details.php?fk_linkcatID=2.

- *Teach them some history.* Many churched college-age people are swayed from the faith with which they were raised because they lack an understanding of Christianity's historical roots. The search for truth through religion usually consists of looking into the history of that particular religious system. The lack of emphasis Christians—Protestants in particular—place on our historical tradition only reinforces the secular message that Christianity can't stand up to scrutiny. The more well-versed that college-age people are on the rich history of our faith, the better they can withstand the pressures to dismiss it as useless.

Guiding college-age people through all the different stages of worldview development takes patience, steadfastness, gentleness, and firmness. Eventually, most will come to a point where they "land" on some conclusions. But our job isn't done when they've reached this point. In fact, it's only just begun.

LANDING ON TRUTH

The process of developing a worldview is long, arduous, and filled with lots of gray areas. But once college-age people come to conclusions about their worldview, things suddenly become black-and-white again; few are willing to compromise on what they now see as truth. Consequently, late adolescents tend to approach conversations with an idealistic, judgmental, and arrogant attitude. I've even come up with a formula to describe it: Knowledge minus experience equals arrogance.

Not long ago, I was at an all-day retreat with our church staff and board. It included everyone from the facilities manager to the administrative staff to interns, pastors, and elders. We had some fun playing dodgeball (always a hit at staff events), ate lunch, and then sat down to talk about our vision for the church. Earlier, our elders had suggested that for one month, the entire church staff use one-third of their paid time to focus solely on prayer. We planned to spend this part of our retreat talking through the logistics of this plan.

At some point in the afternoon, one of our pastors asked for more discussion and feedback about the idea itself. That's when one of our interns made a shocking—and humiliating— statement. He began, "I'm just thankful to God for this." Okay, that sentiment was the good part. But then he kept going. "I've been praying with a group of friends that this church would be more prayer-centered. We've begged God to make our church put their money where their mouth is. So, I'm just thankful the elders realize the need, too."

Yep, he said it out loud. That was what he felt, and it came out.

Now, what he said was kind of true. Our church had been talking a lot about prayer, but we weren't really putting time and energy into it like we should've been. The elder board had been realizing this inconsistency and decided to make some changes to put a greater emphasis on praying into our life as a staff. So the intern hadn't said something untrue. He'd just given himself— and his friends—full credit for getting this issue on the table.

So, we fired the intern (just kidding). But some of us did talk—gently—with him about the comment. He realized what he said and admitted it was an arrogant statement made out of "youthfulness" (his word). Statements like this one aren't uncommon with college-age people. They have ideals about how things ought to run (sometimes the correct ones), but they lack experience. They haven't lived through the pains and joys of trying to implement their ideologies, so they lack patience and don't understand the need for a process. To put it another way, the ideological conclusions to which they come—and the fact that they've never lived them out—cause an arrogant questioning of leadership and authority. Even when their idea of truth is correct, they typically don't approach implementing that truth with maturity.

We have to share with them different perspectives based on experience and biblical truths. We must model humility and submission. We have to hear them out, pay attention to their ideas, and affirm and encourage them in appropriate ways, but not let them get too far down the road of ideological arrogance. This response will, of course, take patience. They'll make stupid comments. They'll have ideas that make total sense to them but can't possibly work in the real world. We have to hear them out, listen in humility, and sometimes even go with what they're saying.

Their inexperience is yet another reason why we must walk them through this entire stage of life. They're seeking truth; but even if they find it, they lack the maturity to handle it appropriately. Helping them come to biblically mature conclusions about truth involves far more than ideology. They can know all the right answers and say all the right words, but embracing those answers and living out their implications is an entirely different step. We can't rush them toward the life they need to live. But we can help them process their search for truth and seek out how to apply that truth.

SECTION THREE
Creating an Effective Ministry

CHAPTER 8

THE LEADER

My first day as a college pastor was interesting, to say the least. I started on a Tuesday morning right after Labor Day. I'd just moved to town that weekend and felt a bit out of place. But I was excited about this church and the potential for this new ministry I'd been asked to start.

I arrived at the church, found the senior pastor's office, and knocked. I didn't know him very well at this point, so I still felt pretty intimidated by him. He called for me to come in, so I opened the door, walked over to shake his hand, and sat down across the desk from him, trying all the while not to let my anxiety show. Once we got past the small talk, I thought we'd move into his thoughts on the college ministry I'd be developing. I assumed that he'd have some pretty clear ideas about what he hoped for, that he'd be as excited about my being there as I was. Instead, he offered some vague suggestion about needing "something" for the college-age people there.

Well, I thought, *at least there are "people."* Then he handed me a little blue Post-it Note with six names on it—the only six college-age people he knew of at the church. As he handed the note to me, he said, "Here you go. Now you can start a college ministry." That was it. No more conversation, no more explanation, no more training or coaching. Just a little list of names.

I'd never done college ministry before, so I didn't have a clue where to start. And he obviously wasn't going to help me figure it out. To add to this "loving encounter," he walked me down to the end of a hallway and pointed to a small table and a chair. He told me I could work there for now and that if I needed to make calls, I could ask someone else if I could use their office phone. Then he walked back to his office and closed the door.

Now that this pastor and I are friends—close friends, in fact—I know he was trying to see what I'd do without direction. And since I served at this church for nine years, I guess I did something right. Still, for the first several months, I felt as though I was walking down a very dark and lonely road.

In retrospect, I was one of the lucky ones. I was at a church that actually saw the need for a specific ministry for college-age people and created a staff position to make it happen. But the longer I've been involved in college-age ministry, the more I realize it's often a back-burner ministry at best, one that doesn't get much attention from the church leadership. That indifference leaves leaders like us wandering, unsure of our role and our mission.

While I can't tell you how to navigate your specific situation, I can offer some general principles for developing an effective ministry. I've discovered most of these ideas the hard way—by making painful mistakes and figuring out how to recover from them. My hope is that by sharing these seven principles with you, I can help you avoid making the same mistakes I made, prepare you for some of the surprises I've faced, show you how to focus on the right areas while staying away from the wrong ones, and point you toward a meaningful mission as you work to create a college-age ministry.

PRINCIPLE #1: BE PEOPLE-DRIVEN, NOT PROGRAM-DRIVEN.

The first time I met Leif, he was drunk. For some reason, God softened my heart toward Leif, and I initiated a friendship with him. I got to know him and started hanging out with him at least once a week. To see the change in his life over the last 10 years has been one of the biggest blessings in my ministry by far.

Leif has told me I was the first person he met from church who "didn't want anything" from him. This impression was a big deal to him. Leif plays the drums very well, so whenever people called him from the church, it was because they wanted him to play for some event or service. Many Sunday mornings, he played drums in church with his belly still full of beer from the night before. Nobody knew this because, well, nobody seemed to care. He played drums, and the service needed a drummer; therefore, he played—no matter what he was going through. After a while, this situation wore on him. He got frustrated and almost left the church.

The leader of a college-age ministry must have a heart for serving people. Some will say they're out to minister to people; but the truth is, they're trying to build a program. Let me put this next statement as bluntly as I can: If you're there for the people in your ministry, then you and your ministry will thrive. If you've got another agenda, then the young people will leave, and your ministry will fail.

As church leaders, we're all a little guilty of meeting with people because of what we can get out of them. If we're honest about it, our motivation for ministry often looks—at least in part—like this:

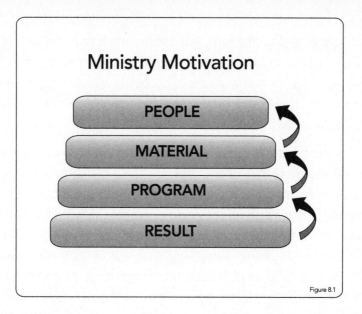

Figure 8.1

The most common question I get from other leaders when they call me about our ministry is something like, "I hear good things are going on over there. What sort of things are you doing?" They see or hear of a "result" (usually the number of people in the ministry), and they want to reproduce it. They assume that if they use our program and our material (the tools we use to make the program work), they can duplicate our success. The thought process is, *If we have what they have, then we can do what they do and therefore produce what they produce.* The motivation isn't ministering to young people. It's trying to get people to show up.

Of course, some people-oriented motivations are mixed into this scenario—I believe they still desire to impact college-age people—but we have to be honest about this unhealthy process. This program-driven way of thinking is repulsive to college-age people who are hungry for authenticity and honesty. When they suspect an agenda—and they are very perceptive about this—they check out. That's why Leif came so close to leaving our church. He felt like he was being used for some other agenda. It's not that people didn't like him; but for the most part, he was right. If we're going to be effective in college-age ministry, then we have to judge that effectiveness by our level of maturity when it comes to developing our college-age people, not the number of people in the room.

Let me be clear: I don't think programming is bad—we want our ministries to be meaningful and well thought out. And of course we want to reach as many people as possible with our ministry. There's also no reason to re-create the wheel, especially when we don't have a clue what we're doing. If one college-age ministry is doing something that seems to really connect with its people, then obviously other ministries shouldn't ignore it if they think it will be meaningful in their groups as well. I believe God calls us to help one another in ministry. (Otherwise I wouldn't have written this book!)

However, we need to pay attention to our motivations, continually asking ourselves where our hearts are. If you're biding your time in college-age ministry until a "real" pastoral job comes along, you need to rethink your motives. If you're looking for praise from your supervisor or book deals from publishers who want to know more about your great ideas, you need to rethink your motives. If your top priority isn't guiding college-age people through what might be the most challenging stage of their lives, you need to rethink your motives. College-age people—perhaps more than any other age group—need you to be invested in them. Quite simply, that personal engagement is what ministry to this group looks like.

PRINCIPLE #2: DON'T LET STRUCTURE
GET IN THE WAY OF RELATIONSHIPS.

Even the most people-oriented ministries can fail if they're overly structured. If you've come out of a youth ministry background, then you probably learned that more structure can equal greater effectiveness. But while college-age people need some structure, they really want relationships. And often, structure gets in the way of relationships.

One of the ways we tend to over-structure is by constantly creating events. Effective college-age ministry isn't event-driven. Instead, it revolves naturally around people and relationships. Our tendency is to put together events in order to help people get to know one another. This approach can work for a while, but I've found that college-age people prefer to cultivate relationships on a daily basis, rather than monthly or quarterly. College-age ministry functions best not by holding events for the purpose of building relationships, but by cultivating relationships that create the events.

I've learned that the traditional big push for a new ministry element—small groups, for example—will get a fairly decent response upfront. But over time the enthusiasm wears off. The reason is that it was promoted as a relational event—they'd get to know others and grow closer to God. This connection is what they want, so they give it a try. But then they get involved, don't connect with the leader or with others in the group, and drop out. The group has become little more than an obligation, and they don't need any more pressure to be places they don't want to be. What started off as a desire to be relational and to grow in faith turned into religious routine.

Instead, I've found it most effective to offer very informal opportunities for connection—communal meals, informal conversations at a coffee shop, movie nights, study sessions—whatever provides just enough structure to get people together without getting in the way of naturally forming relationships.

PRINCIPLE #3: BE PREPARED TO HANDLE MAJOR THEOLOGICAL DISCUSSIONS.

College-age people are often very interested in the more complex issues of theology. While some are very simplistic in their understanding of and approach to faith, many are anxious to dive into the deeper theological debates that have been going on for centuries—usually with the belief that they'll be the ones to find the answer. Although this process can be healthy and necessary for many college-age people, it can lead others into some dangerous spiritual waters. Leading a college-age ministry demands discernment on the part of leaders as we determine whether or not our students are moving through this process in a healthy manner, one person at a time.

I've had college-age people ask questions that range from "What does it mean to be a Christian?" to "How do I know if I'm a dispensationalist or a covenantalist?" The spectrum is incredibly diverse when it comes to college-age people and their knowledge of the Bible and theology. Leaders need to be prepared to address this entire spectrum.

You don't have to have all the answers. In fact, the best leaders have the humility to admit when issues are over their heads. Often, our *not* knowing can create an even greater opportunity for ministry than having an answer. When we don't know, we can spend time finding the answer alongside the people who are asking. Not only can we model healthy theological exploration, but we also get the chance to learn about the people themselves—how they think and process and where they are in their understanding of faith.

Whether you're just getting started in college-age ministry or have been at it for a few years, make sure you're always pursuing theological understanding yourself. Read, talk to other Christians, and know the historical issues and debates and where you stand on them. Not only will it help you address the questions of your college-age people, but it will help your faith grow as well.

PRINCIPLE #4: KNOW HOW TO COUNSEL PEOPLE IN PAIN.

We can all point to extremely painful times in our lives when we learned significant lessons. While we wish we could have avoided some of them, others we wouldn't change for the world. The college-age years are full of these times. All of the issues we discussed in the previous section of the book—identity, intimacy, meaning, pleasure, truth—create a great deal of internal pain and confusion. As leaders, we'll have more conversations about these issues than we ever imagined. And we need to be ready to offer compassion, understanding, sympathy, and prayer along with our guidance.

I remember sitting down with Gabe for the first time. He was so absorbed in his search for identity that he could hardly figure out what he wanted in life. In fact, his thoughts were so overwhelming that he couldn't even articulate what they were. He was facing pressures from family, relational tensions with friends, and financial issues with his education. In addition to all these external stressors, he was trying to examine his own motivations and determine what he thought he should do with his life. He was at a point of total frustration. This confusion is the norm for college-age people. It's no wonder they welcome our help.

During the college-age years, young people begin to look at themselves in a more introspective way. They're truly taking stock of who they are, and as they do, they're often confronted with parts of themselves they don't like. They start thinking not only about how they feel, but also about why they feel that way. And that self-examination can bring up painful issues. They might start rethinking an incident with a parent or sibling that caused them great pain and find themselves dealing with the emotional fallout of that incident. They might realize the pain they caused others while they were growing up and struggle with what it means to be responsible for those actions. They might bring up past trauma or fears that they've never talked about before. There's no telling what college-age people will discover when they think about themselves in deeper, abstract ways.

Leaders must be able to listen to these stories without saying too much. College-age people need to think through these issues, not wade through a mountain of advice and answers. Verbalizing their thoughts to a trustworthy person is perhaps the best way for them to process what they're thinking and feeling. We stunt that process when we tell them what's right or wrong about what they feel. An effective leader asks questions that help people think through their issues from a biblical perspective.

Naturally, if you feel you're in over your head, bring in help. There's no shame in not knowing how to help someone who's in a genuine crisis. If a college-age person comes to you with a story that's just too much for you to handle, get her connected with a Christian counselor or person in your church who, through personal experience, can give more significant help.

PRINCIPLE #5: BE HONEST, EVEN WHEN IT HURTS.

If there's one thing college-age people appreciate, it's honesty and bluntness. When they know we love them, they have great respect for us when we speak the hard truth to them with grace and understanding. They want to know what we're thinking, and they know instinctively when we're not being straight with them. This candor is a large part of our work in helping them mature. If someone is caught up in her selfishness and pride, then she needs people she trusts to tell her what they see. If a person is contradicting himself in his beliefs (which will happen frequently in late adolescence), then he needs someone to point it out. Obviously, these conversations can take place only after you've developed a relationship with your college-age people. But sugarcoating issues comes across as phony, even if a relationship hasn't been established yet.

I've been surprised by how often college-age people who've been involved in our ministry will come back and tell me it was the hard, pointed conversations I had with them that made the biggest impact. It wasn't the messages I gave from the stage (although I would love for them to say that sometime!); it was the conversations we had over cups of coffee or during long walks that stand out for them. They tell me those times are when they felt the most cared for.

We can write great sermons. We can plan fantastic events. We can run smooth programs. But if we aren't willing to walk through the difficult conversations that help our college-age people grow, then we're failing in ministry.

PRINCIPLE #6: WORK WITH OLDER ADULTS.

One of the primary goals of a college-age ministry is to bridge the gap between the youth-group years and the "adult" ministry years. So part of our job as leaders is to create a process of assimilation that helps college-age people invest themselves in the life of the church. I find that integration happens most naturally when we build relationships between college-age people and older people in the church.

Those relationships, however, won't just happen by themselves. Leaders need to create opportunities for older Christians to connect with college-age people. Meet with and personally ask older people to serve as mentors for college-age people. As leaders, we need to be the ones who initiate these relationships. And the stronger your relationships in the community, the more your college-age people will want to echo those relationships in their lives. The added benefit is that you can discover common interests or experiences between older people and your college-age people. If you know Bob the lawyer loves to read philosophy, introduce him to Mike, the philosophy major. Be the bridge builder between the generations, and you'll help your college-age people flow into the church community with far less effort.

PRINCIPLE #7: UNDERSTAND AND WORK WITH THE CHURCH STRUCTURE.

Understanding how college-age ministry functions within the broader church is crucial to the effectiveness of the ministry. That knowledge involves understanding what kind of overall vision drives the church. For example, if you've got a missions mindset but your church sees itself as a local-outreach community, then you're going to find yourself constantly running into ideological—

not to mention financial—roadblocks. If you want the staff and congregation to support your ministry, then you need to be in tune with what has drawn those people to this community.

This understanding is also a crucial aspect of the assimilation process I mentioned above. You want to guide your college-age people toward life in the church. That direction doesn't just mean making sure they're comfortable at a church service, but ensuring that they understand the overall function of a Christian community as well. Right now, they'll likely limit their involvement to your ministry. But the hope is that they'll eventually see themselves as a vital part of the greater body and seek out ways to use their gifts in the life of the church. If they've been isolated from the overall vision of the church, they're in for a rude awakening when they move out of the college-age ministry.

An effective college-age ministry depends on an effective leader. These seven principles of leadership will help you avoid the common pitfalls of leadership—and believe me, you want to avoid them at all costs. But they aren't the only guidance we need as leaders. We don't just need to develop solid ministries; we need to develop ourselves as well.

WHAT MAKES A LEADER?

There's more to leadership than just doing the right things. It's essential for a college-age-ministry leader to model the character we hope our college-age people will develop. That need might seem obvious, but I'm often stunned by the lack of leadership I see in college-age ministers. I believe many of them underestimate the level of maturity needed to truly shepherd college-age people. By now, you know college-age ministry isn't an extension of youth group. But far too many leaders see it that way. They figure they just have to provide some fun activities, put together some events, and help college-age people bide their time until they can get involved in "real" church activities.

But college-age people need and long for so much more. And they can't find something deeper unless we're committed to taking our leadership role seriously. Being effective means developing the true character of a leader. We can define that character in a number of ways, but I believe every leader needs six characteristics in particular to be effective.

1. Be a seeker of discipline. We can't help others embrace this concept unless we do first. If we expect our college-age people to be disciplined in their lives, then we must be the same. We don't discipline ourselves for the sake of being a good role model, but for the sake of shepherding well. We need to know how to manage our time, how to balance our lives so we'll have the energy and time for our ministry. We need to spend time in prayer and study so we'll keep our own faith alive. We need to seek out fellowship so we'll be nurtured by a community. We don't have to be perfect. In fact, understanding where we're weak, knowing what our struggles are, and seeking out the help we need is also a form of self-discipline.

College-age people often ask me and our other adult volunteers how we manage our day, schedule our time, handle responsibilities—even budget our money. If we haven't been figuring out the answers, we can't be much help to them.

2. Gain perspective on the pursuit of pleasure. Just as our college-age people look to us to show them what a disciplined life looks like, they also look to us to see what it means to enjoy the life God gave us. I appreciate what King Solomon says about pleasure in the book of Ecclesiastes. He speaks of balancing temporal and immediate pleasures with an eternal perspective. He says to enjoy life and follow our hearts, but also remember that all these pursuits will one day be brought before God (Ecclesiastes 11:9). He concludes his writing by proclaiming that the point of being alive is to honor God and keep God's commandments (Ecclesiastes 12:13-14). There's nothing wrong with enjoying life—God wants that for us. But we enjoy life by pursuing God, not our selfish desires.

Here again, our example not only shows our college-age people how to strike the balance between fun and discipline, but it also helps us do our work well. Plenty of times, we'll feel more like hanging out with our friends than with college-age people. At times we'll want to sleep late instead of heading off to a breakfast meeting. But we must have the maturity to balance the fun in our lives with the discipline we need in order to do what we've been called to do.

3. Realize the need for Christ. Hopefully, everyone reading this book knows that we each need Christ. But I find it's easy to forget about the role Christ plays in our ministry. College-age ministry can be full of ego. It's great to have a deep conversation with someone and feel as though you've really helped that person through a rough time. But we need to always remember that apart from Christ, we simply don't have the ability to change anyone—especially with respect to faith, hope, and love.

We're the tools God uses, and we can't get caught up in our performance. We can help college-age people think through issues from a biblical perspective, push them toward Scripture for guidance, and model godliness in our personal lives, but God will be the one who changes them. Not only is this actually the case, but keeping it in your mind will also help you avoid the frustration that's so often part of discipling college-age people—especially those who never seem to get it. You can't force others to embrace the concepts you're trying to instill in them, but you can model them and trust that God is working on the hearts of these people, too.

4. Truly love college-age people. This statement may seem obvious, but it's easy to forget what love really looks like. First Corinthians 13 lists the characteristics of love, and the very first one is patience. Far too often, people in college-age ministry live with intense frustration toward their group members. That lack of patience can lead to other kinds of "loveless" attitudes, such as rudeness and an arrogance that insists on its own way. Love speaks truth and doesn't laugh at wrongdoings. Love doesn't get irritable or resentful when people don't follow instruction. Love never fails to be there when needed. Biblical love is the most important part of discipleship in a college-age person's life. And if the love for college-age people isn't there, then you'll never be able to endure the years it takes for discipleship.

5. Reveal the pleasure of faithfulness. The truth is, more pleasure is in giving than receiving (Acts 20:35). As our college-age friends seek out pleasure, we can show them how we're finding pleasure and blessing through service. Tell them how you feel when you help someone. Talk about mission trips or service work you've done and what those experiences have meant to you. Then provide opportunities for them to serve—mission trips, community outreach, working in the church nursery, or visiting the elderly. Encourage their ideas for service opportunities and help them process what they experience.

6. Show consistency. Late adolescence is all about inconsistency, so we need to be doubly consistent. We need to show up on time (or early!) for appointments with college-age people. We need to follow through on commitments we make to them. We have to model adult-like consistency for our people because these seemingly small gestures often have the biggest impact. When we're consistent in their lives, they'll notice. And they'll be more grateful than they can say.

Leading a college-age ministry doesn't have to be like walking blind. When we're committed to building an effective ministry that meets the unique needs of college-age people, we'll thrive. It won't always be easy, and you're sure to run into hurdles I never faced. But I hope this chapter will save you some struggles along the way. The bottom line is that college-age people need theologically solid, caring, humble, relational people who are willing to walk alongside them as they mature. If you're that person, then you really can't fail.

CHAPTER 9

THE TEACHING AND DISCIPLESHIP

I love to travel, and in recent years I've had the privilege of visiting a number of places I never dreamed I'd see. I love meeting the people, trying the food, experiencing other ways of thinking about life. No matter where I go, I always discover some odd cultural quirk that reminds me just how much of what we do, think, and believe comes from the culture in which we live. But one experience blew all of the others away.

A few years ago I was in Papua New Guinea speaking at a camp for missionary kids. PNG is a small country just off the shore of Australia. It's a deeply tribal country where more than 800 languages are spoken. When the camp session was over, I had the chance to visit one of the tribal villages with a missionary. We were walking up a trail when the missionary asked if I had a camera. I told him I did, so he asked me to take a picture of a woman up ahead. I agreed and walked up to the little old woman. I showed her my camera as if to ask her if I could take her picture. She nodded, stood up as straight, smiled, and waited for me to take her picture. I snapped the shot, and she immediately leaned over to look at the screen on the back of my camera. I was a little surprised that she knew the camera had a screen, but she'd obviously done this before. She looked at the picture, then looked at me with a huge smile. She was thrilled.

It's not an overstatement to say that what happened next is the weirdest thing I've ever experienced. Looking at me with her ear-to-ear smile, she reached out her right hand and briefly grabbed me in the crotch!

I was completely shocked. Stunned. Confused. Horrified. What just happened?

Not knowing what to do or how to respond, I looked to the missionary for help. But he was no help at all because he was bent over and laughing hysterically. When he stood up, tears were rolling down his face. He could hardly speak, he was laughing so hard. That's when I realized I'd been set up.

When he finally caught his breath, the missionary explained that he arranged for us to "bump into" this woman to illustrate how important it is to understand cultural differences. I got the point; I just wish I hadn't "gotten" the point.

It turns out that in this woman's tribe, this action is the way a woman thanks a man when he does something nice for her. It's considered rude *not* to do it. I asked the missionary why this gesture—out of all the possible ways of saying thank you—was the one they chose. He said, "I don't know. It's just the way they've always done it."

Every "tribe" has its cultural norms. When I was a little boy, my mom told me it was rude to put my elbows on the table when I ate. I asked her why, and she said, "I don't know; it just is." When we grow up with those norms, we rarely question them.

The Christian "tribe" is no different. Like any other culture, Christianity has its norms and expectations and assumptions about how we are to think and live as people of God. Those who grow up in the church rarely question these norms—until they get to be college-age. Then—in the midst of the search for identity and meaning—everything becomes open to question.

If we were only talking about issues such as, "Why do we sit in pews?" or "Why do we dress up for church?" I wouldn't spend a whole chapter talking about how leaders need to deal with these questions. But the issues college-age students want to know about are far more complicated. They're the essential questions of faith—How do I know this is true? What if Jesus was just a man? Why should I choose Christianity over some other religion that seems pretty appealing?

Nearly all college-age people get to the point where they begin to question the faith in which they were raised. We can either answer those questions with the same responses that worked when they were 12, or we can recognize that college-age people are ready for a new way of thinking and learning. If we choose the latter, then we need to be prepared for a new way of teaching.

THE WEAKNESS OF LINEAR TEACHING

When we're growing up, the world is very black-and-white. There is good and there is bad. There is nice and there is naughty. We think that way because our brains process information in a linear fashion: $A + B = C$. But by late adolescence, the brain is able to process information in nonlinear, abstract ways—it can recognize that sometimes $A + B = Q$.

Not only is there room for ambiguity, but the maturing brain *expects* ambiguity as well. In other words, college-age people are able to handle abstract concepts and they're no longer satisfied with simplified answers to what they believe are complex questions. That's good news because it means they're ready and excited to dig into their faith in ways they never could before.

It also means we need to understand why linear thinking limits the spiritual growth of college-age people. I want to be careful here because I know for some people, this kind of talk can be scary. It may sound as though I'm suggesting we avoid speaking about truth or sound doctrine. I'm not. I'm suggesting that we think about how we articulate truth and that we honor the process which college-age people must go through in order to discover truth on their own. When we say God is this or that but we can only support that statement by saying, "That's what the Bible says," we're being theologically lazy. A statement can be true but that doesn't mean it's helpful. At some point, a college-age person is going to question this linear logic—and if we're not prepared to engage their questions, we'll lose them.

Our traditional approach to spiritual formation isn't really forming people as much as it is indoctrinating them. The simple articulation of conclusions we've come to doesn't prepare college-age people for the intellectual challenges they'll face as adult Christians.

Let me put it another way. College-age people who were raised with one perspective on questions of identity and meaning and life eventually become aware that this perspective isn't the only way of thinking, that the answer might not have been as simple as the church made it seem. They start to wonder why we never told them about these other perspectives. And then they question all the conclusions we've taught them, wondering if the church is hiding something.

Nurturing the faith of college-age people demands that we leaders break away from offering simple answers to difficult questions. For most of us, that change will mean shifting away from the educational models of spiritual formation that churches have been using for decades and replacing them with a different, more relational model of discipleship.

BREAKING AWAY FROM THE EDUCATIONAL MODEL

When you think about France, you probably don't consider it to be a place where you might learn a lot about spiritual formation. But the French have an interesting approach to education that I believe speaks to the way we need to disciple college-age people.

The French value logic and human reason above all else. The two professions held in highest esteem in French culture are engineers and philosophers because they're seen as critical thinkers, and critical thinking is highly valued; the thought process is far more important than the conclusion. If you were to sit through a church service in France, then you'd notice right away that a different style of education is at work. The pastor would hold firmly to the truth of a biblical passage, yet his message would probably concentrate more on the process of coming to the conclusion than what the conclusion might be. In this method, he challenges the congregation to determine for themselves how they ought to approach understanding the passage. He'd most likely never offer a practical application of the message.

In many American Protestant churches, the exact opposite happens. We expect the pastor to weed through all the options during sermon prep so the sermon is the final word on the subject. Then, because we tend to be results-oriented, we want the pastor to tell us what to do about what we've learned. We want application. To the American mind, this approach makes perfect sense.

For the French, the point of a sermon goes much deeper than a change in behavior. The desire is for personal and communal change in thought. The pastor's goal is to stimulate deeper thinking, not call for an immediate behavioral response.

For college-age people, the typical American approach of boiling down a conclusion to its most digestible points is boring. It feels trite and simplistic. It doesn't provoke thought or engagement. It just creates an expectation that being a Christian means doing the right things. And that result isn't what we want for our college-age people. Instead, we want them to be passionate about thinking correctly, asking questions, and seeking answers for themselves.

To get them there, our approach to discipleship needs to focus on three significant changes in the way we think and talk about faith. If we make these characteristics the hallmarks of our teaching, then our college-age ministries will do more than thrive. They'll launch thoughtful, faithful men and women back into the life of the church. And when that assimilation happens, everyone wins.

FROM TEACHING THE LAW TO TEACHING THE FAITH

When I first started in college-age ministry, I noticed that the disengagement so many college-age people felt wasn't from the people or the work of the church, but from the faith itself. It just didn't make sense to them anymore. So I wanted to find out what they were disengaging from. What were they learning as kids that was no longer meaningful as young adults? To find out, I decided to sit in on a few Sunday school classes.

For six months I sat in a too-small plastic chair and watched what the classes were like, what the leaders were teaching, and how the kids responded to the teaching. I was pleasantly surprised to see kids responding with smiles, laughter, and overall enjoyment. I was also very excited about our volunteers, how committed they were to these kids whom they clearly loved.

But I saw something else that wasn't so pleasant. The teachers were often focusing on the law, not the faith. The classes emphasized behavior over everything else. Don't get me wrong, these teachers were teaching about God, and the behavior emphasis certainly wasn't an effort to hide anything from these kids. But the main thrust of the classes—and I'm talking about preschoolers all the way up to high schoolers—was behavior management.

The applications of the lessons were variations of the same five things: Read your Bible, pray, go to church, invite your friends to church, and obey your parents. In junior and senior high, the leaders added a few others: Share your faith, serve, don't have sex or do drugs. When I asked some of the kids what they were learning about being a Christian, almost all of them defined it as doing or not doing these things. Christianity simply meant following the law.

I also talked to the teachers. The difference between what they *thought* they were teaching and what the kids were *actually* learning was clear. They'd teach abstract concepts about God (personality, character, and so on) and then use practical suggestions to show the kids how these concepts should apply to their lives. But the kids didn't see the connection. Why? Because that's abstract thinking, and kids don't think that way. Instead, they heard a list of dos and don'ts.

When those same kids hit late adolescence, they want more than a list of behaviors. They want reasons for following the law.

They want to know why it matters. They want to know why some of their friends who've done everything "right" still suffered. Or why their heads are full of rules, but they have no real relationship with God. If we leave them in that place of confusion and doubt, they'll disconnect from the church and search for answers somewhere else.

I've seen countless college-age people come to a point where they find that the "boundaries" they were taught in church aren't of God at all. They feel as though the adults in the church too often judge them by what they do, not who they are. And that sense creates confusion and the feeling that the church is hypocritical—there's unconditional love for all, but only if we obey all the rules. I'm not saying the boundaries they learned as children aren't good and healthy. But we have to be very careful about the message we're sending, making it clear that how we live is a reflection of what's happening inside us. We have to emphasize that we're interested in internal growth. We need to reinforce the idea that God wants us to have fulfilling lives, and boundaries can help us realize that fulfillment.

College-age people need us to replace what they've heard about a legalistic faith with a new covenant faith, the kind Jesus ushered in. The new covenant wasn't about rules. It was just the opposite. In Colossians 2:20-23 Paul writes,

> Since you died with Christ to the elemental spiritual forces of this world, why, as though you still belonged to the world, do you submit to its rules: 'Do not handle! Do not taste! Do not touch!'? These rules, which have to do with things that are all destined to perish with use, are based on merely human commands and teachings. Such regulations indeed have an appearance of wisdom, with their self-imposed

worship, their false humility and their harsh treatment of the body, but they lack any value in restraining sensual indulgence."

While we want our college-age people to live godly, disciplined lives, we want them to do so out of their sense of who they are in God, their sense of meaning and purpose, and their desire to live the lives God intended for them. College-age people are hungry for the deeper aspects of faith. So we need to move away from just talking through concrete and behavioral issues and move toward abstract issues in Scripture. For instance, in Ephesians 1:1-14 Paul writes about who we are spiritually (abstract thoughts). Instead of telling your college-age people what spiritual identity looks like from a behavior perspective, help them think through the implications of being the people Paul says we are. Ask questions, get them thinking, and don't worry if they can't come up with something concrete. The point is engagement, not answers.

FROM KNOWING FACTS
TO UNDERSTANDING TRUTH

James was a guy in my college ministry. He was a great kid and well liked by everyone. We were sitting down for coffee one day, and he told me straight out that he was bored with God and with church. He wasn't bitter or frustrated; he was just being honest. I asked him why he thought he was bored, and he simply responded, "I'm just sick of going to church."

Eventually, James explained that his entire Christian life revolved around the church campus where Bible studies were held and church events hosted. He was saturated by church culture and knew a lot of biblical information. He went from one Bible study or gathering to the next, and eventually he got bored—who wouldn't? At the same time, he was living his life by his own rules. He wasn't doing anything particularly awful, but he wasn't living a Christlike life either. Like so many college-age people, he was following his own desires, not God's.

At the end of our conversation, I looked him straight in the eyes and said, "You're right—your life is boring. Your problem is that you're a smart guy and you know a lot of information, but you don't obey any of it." I'm not always that forward with people, but our relationship warranted it, and he certainly needed to hear it. I went on, "I wonder if it would be so boring if you started living out what you know—if you were able to say you knew things from experience, rather than just repeating what you've been told?" He was a little taken aback, but he understood what I was saying. If he wanted his faith to mean something, he needed to move it out of his head and into his heart.

Teaching straight information about our faith certainly has its place. The early church listened to the apostles' teachings, Christ commanded his disciples to teach everything he'd told them, and Paul commands Timothy and Titus to teach sound doctrine as pastors. It's clearly important for Christians to know the basics of what it means to be a person of faith. But college-age people aren't interested in more information. They don't need more facts to help them hold on to their faith or stay involved in the church.

College-age people are generally bored with church, especially when they're force-fed information that seems one-sided and overly simplistic. Those who've grown up in church feel as though they've heard it all (which, of course, they haven't), they've processed it all (which, of course, they haven't), and they're ready to explore other avenues that deal with faith issues (which, of course, they are). If the church doesn't encourage this desire to know more and think more deeply, we'll leave them believing there's nothing more to know.

But they know that's not the case. College-age people will inevitably find friends or coworkers or college professors who *have* thought more deeply about the big questions of life, and they'll be pulled away from the church and toward those who seem to be having a far more stimulating conversation.

For some college-age people, this process of learning and discovery is fascinating. But for others, it's shattering. Their worldview is unraveling in a college classroom, and no one is there to help them work through all of the upheaval that unraveling causes.

As leaders, we need to initiate the process of moving our college-age people into a place where more thought is required of them. It's not enough for us to catch them when they fall apart at college. We need to be the *first* ones to say, "This faith of ours deserves deeper thought. Let's dig in together." This discipleship entails helping college-age people learn to think for themselves, challenging thought processes, and helping them think about the world through a biblical grid. We must encourage deeper commitment to and understanding of the simple—and sometimes not-so-simple—truths of Scripture.

FROM SURFACE ASSUMPTIONS TO DEEPER CONNECTIONS

Those of us who've been Christians for a long time sometimes forget that underneath every truth we cling to are layers of belief. For example, I believe Jesus Christ is God in the flesh and the only way to the Father. But below the surface of this belief are a whole host of other beliefs. For me to believe Jesus is God-made-flesh, I first need to assume that God exists. I also have to assume that the God of the universe is in fact the same God I read about in the Bible. I need to believe the Bible to be true and trustworthy.

I have to believe that the specific translation of the Bible I use is an accurate articulation of the original writings. And I have to believe those writings report actual events. Clearly, a lot of pre-suppositions are beneath every "fact" we hold as truth.

When I say college-age people are ready to go deeper, I'm talking about this layered belief system. They don't need us to convince them that Jesus is the Son of God. They need us to walk with them as they peel back all the presuppositions and explore all the assumptions behind that belief.

That exploration isn't a bad thing. In fact, I would argue it's a necessary thing.

When we focus on conclusions (the surface) and then move directly to application (behavior), we rob college-age people of an entire maturation process. As teachers, we have to be the catalyst to deeper thinking about the assumptions behind the conclusions. If we don't have this approach, then we're essentially assuming that college-age people have the same presuppositions we have. And while some may share those presuppositions and will continue to do so, the majority of college-age people are reevaluating and questioning their previous assumptions. I've found this fact to be as true of those who grew up in the church as it is of those who didn't. So it seems ridiculous—and arrogant—to negate their thought processes and focus solely on behavioral application that's based on *our* assumptions and conclusions.

It's not wrong to declare our beliefs to those with whom we work. In fact, we should. It's not wrong to talk about how our beliefs play out in our lives in practical ways. Sharing about our own faith experiences can be helpful to college-age people. But we have to remember that we arrived at these beliefs because we took the time to work through the layers of assumptions behind them. We need to guide our college-age people through that same experience.

DIFFICULT QUESTIONS AND AMBIGUOUS ANSWERS

Sometimes we just want answers, practical application, or some-one to flat-out tell us what to do. Take, for instance, the encoun-ter Jesus has with the Pharisees in Matthew 22:34-37. In Jesus' day the religous leaders had divided the Old Testament Law into 613 separate laws. Of those, 248 were considered positive and 365 negative; they had a whole system figured out. Since they had all these different divisions and rankings, they assumed Jesus would have a system as well. So by asking him what he thought the greatest commandment was, they were essentially asking, "What's the most important thing we ought to be doing?" It wasn't that they really wanted to know. They wanted to find out if Jesus agreed with them.

In response, Jesus quotes a passage of Scripture found in Deu-teronomy 6:4-9 known as the *Shema* (Hebrew word for "hear"). Faithful Jews recited this passage at least twice a day, every day. The religious leaders copied this text onto small pieces of parch-ment, put them in little cases, and wore them on their foreheads and left arms (in the armpit area) during times of prayer. This custom was part of their religious routine. In Matthew 23:5 Jesus actually rebukes people for wearing these Scripture boxes because they were trying to look "holy." The Pharisees would also put this passage in *mezuzahs* (small boxes) and place them on all the doorposts in their home, excluding the bathroom and possibly kitchen (those places were deemed unsanitary). Needless to say, they were very familiar with the passage Jesus quotes.

Jesus' response in Matthew 22:37 of, "Love the Lord your God with all your heart and with all your soul and with all your mind," was a subversive answer on a number of levels. In this response, Jesus points out that the highest Law isn't something a person can just do. It's an ambiguous answer to a concrete question. You can't prove that someone is loving God with all her heart, soul, and mind. You can't quantify it. It's not really a practical expression of faith because it doesn't look like any one behavior.

But Jesus was also telling the Pharisees that they'd missed the very point of this passage they recited every day, carried on their bodies, and nailed to their houses. They'd literally carried the message with them as an act of faithfulness without actually embedding that message in their hearts.

Teaching college-age people has to move beyond practical application and simple conclusions played out in religous routine. They know right from wrong, nice from naughty. They need to know why it matters. We have to guide them as they think beyond actions and behaviors. Not doing so misses the very core of discipleship.

CHAPTER 10

THE GATHERING

Hi, my name is Yanet, and I'm part of a leadership team of a college-age group in Chicago. I'm new at this and was looking for resources and came across your blog. There's not much out there for college-age ministry, but I'm glad someone is starting to do something. Our church has around 26 college students; some are actively involved in ministry, but the majority are transitioning from youth group (recent high school graduates), and it's been really hard to get the group to join in on what we're doing. Out of the 26 people, maybe five show up to our Bible study. We want this to change and are open to any ideas—thought maybe you could help?

I get emails like this one almost every day. Although they ask in different ways, most of the people who write to me want to know the same thing: How do we get people to show up? As more and more churches recognize the need for some kind of college-age ministry, these requests will just keep coming. While I love to help new ministries get started, and while I know there's a terrible lack of resources for college-age ministry, I'm always nervous about articulating the "program" side of our of what we do. As I discussed in chapter 8, we leaders sometimes find it easier to re-create something God has already done somewhere else and through someone else than to start from scratch ourselves. Believe me, if I could have turned to some transferable ministry model when I started, I probably would have jumped on it. But nothing was out there.

So instead, I spent a lot of time on my knees, talking to God and asking for inspiration and help. My prayers were often, "Lord, I don't have a clue what I'm doing, so I really need you to do something!" And really, that's where every ministry should start—with prayer. I find that whenever I get comfortable with what I'm doing or feel like we've got some momentum going in the ministry, the less I rely on God to inspire and guide me. So I'll issue this disclaimer: I will share some key lessons I've learned that I believe could be beneficial to your ministry, but I won't list out 10 things you should or shouldn't do. If you're still interested, keep reading.

WORKING WITHOUT A NET

Nearly every person I meet who's thinking of starting a college-age ministry has the same initial idea: Start with a weekly gathering of some kind. That idea sounds like a great start, but I want to encourage you to do anything *but* start with a weekly gathering.

The beauty of a college-age ministry is that it can—and should—look like anything, maybe like nothing else in the church. Getting out of the traditional ministry mindset is the first step to being successful in college-age ministry. Unlike other ministries, college-age ministry needs to be organic. Why? Because relationships are naturally that way, and relationships are vital in our ministry. If growing your ministry organically means spending months just having one-on-one conversations with college-age people, so be it. If it means explaining to the senior pastor over and over that you really are working even though you're rarely in the office, that's okay.

I meet people all the time who invite college-age people into their homes, investing in them, helping them think through issues—and yet they feel they're not doing enough. It doesn't feel like "real" ministry to them. They couldn't be more wrong! The feeling that they should be doing more comes from the programmatic mindset that's so pervasive in churches. But the effectiveness of college-age ministry isn't about big programs or flashy events. It's about people.

Regardless of the size of your program, church, or budget, your ministry can thrive. You don't need some tried-and-true curriculum or format developed at a church that looks nothing like yours. Instead, you need to focus on four areas that make a college-age ministry the kind of place that college-age people want to be. And whether you have 5 of them or 500 of them, college-age people will mature as individuals and as Christians if you teach in a way that engages the mind and develop strong community, effective worship, and a relationship-based atmosphere. We've already looked at the teaching piece, so in this chapter I'll walk you through the other three gathering points.

BUILDING COMMUNITY

It's no secret that college-age people are all about social connections. The loss of identity that comes after they leave high school instills a desire for relationships like never before. If they don't find relationships in one place, they'll move on to another. Our gatherings need to emphasize community connections. Whether it's a planned element during an evening of other events, extra time at the end of a gathering, a coffeehouse setting, or simply informal groups grabbing a meal, it's important to provide opportunities for friendships to form. The typical church-service approach of having people briefly greet each other before they sit down doesn't do it. College-age people need to have open-ended time for conversation and connection.

At the same time, college-age ministries have to be more than social clubs. We can add deeper meaning to relationship-building in two ways: First, by helping them see that their desire for relationships is God-designed, and second, by making community-building a primary part of the ministry. Infusing spiritual significance into your ministry means going beyond just tacking on some extra time for conversation to the end of a gathering. Instead, make community an act of worship. Many times we feel like if we don't pray, have a Bible study, or include some other formal "churchy" element, then we're not doing anything distinctly Christian. That reasoning simply isn't true. Instead of singing praise songs or giving a talk, create time for people to just hang out with no other agenda. Make it clear that celebrating the relationships God gives us *is* worship.

Encouraging deep and intimate relationships in our ministries has tremendous benefits; however, that strong desire to develop close relationships can also lead college-age people to shut out newcomers or those they don't click with. One of the biggest struggles in the early days of our ministry was making sure people were aware of others outside the core group. When we were a small group, everyone seemed open to building new relationships. But when we hit 30 people or so, the group dynamic shifted. We'd developed a personality that felt comfortable for those who'd been there for a while, but that familiarity made it difficult for new people to feel welcome.

During one of our first leadership-team meetings, I had everyone stand in a circle. I told them to put a hand on the shoulder of the person on either side of them. As we looked at each other, I said, "Isn't it awesome to have a group of people like this who you can trust and live life with?" Everyone agreed. It was a cool moment—but not a healthy one. We liked it this way—knowing each other and feeling safe together. But that security wasn't the purpose of our ministry. So I asked everyone to put their hands back down and turn around so we were facing outside of the circle. I then asked them to once again put a hand on the shoulder of the person on either side of them.

My point was that we could still be close, still have community, and still reach out to others around us. Our group needed to understand that building community with each other wasn't the end goal—it was a means to a much greater goal. Small groups of people are often afraid to reach out to others. They worry that new people will compromise their intimacy with one another. But I find the opposite to be true: Groups grow stronger when they continue reaching out, together.

Finding the balance between socializing and ministry isn't easy. But it's essential that we find it. If we let our ministry be solely social, we risk becoming inauthentic. If a visitor's perception of the ministry is that it's simply a social gathering, it's not going to be attractive. Most college-age people come to church because they want friendships *and* spiritual formation. It's our job to find and keep that balance. Now, I wouldn't necessarily recommend doing what I did to keep the balance, but I'll tell you about it anyway.

We initially started holding our gathering times on Thursday nights in a classroom at our church. (I know I said not to start with a weekly gathering. I warned against it because I know better now.) The first night, nearly 20 people showed up, and after about eight weeks, our group had more than doubled in size. I noticed the social aspect of the ministry was moving extremely fast—in many ways, it had become the draw. So one week when I got up to speak, I ended up throwing out my talk. Instead, I sat on a stool and simply poured out my heart. I talked about how much I valued relationships and said I was encouraged by how well people were getting to know one another.

But then I explained the purpose of this ministry—and it wasn't to be a social club. We wanted to reach people for the purpose of presenting them complete in Christ (Colossians 1:28). I explained that I wouldn't allow this ministry to become nothing more than a social avenue for them. I said if our ministry became just a social get-together, I would shut it down. I said all of this very bluntly—I probably could've handled it more gently. But I was concerned.

You should've seen the looks on their faces. I killed a sacred cow that I didn't even know existed. I had no idea how important relationships were to them, and if I had, I probably would've been a little more patient. But not too much more. The way a ministry starts off sets the pace for its future. I could have articulated my thoughts differently, but I meant what I said—and I didn't care if people left. Which was good, because they did leave.

Two weeks after my talk, our attendance had dropped to 19 people, including myself and the worship leaders! It was hard, and I got some serious criticism from some church staff members. I even second-guessed what I did at times. But looking back, I'm extremely thankful for that night. From then on, we had a good balance and a solid core of people who understood what we were about.

I'm almost certain my approach wasn't the best way to achieve balance for our ministry, but I share the story with you to point out how seriously we have to take this issue. Once the social aspect takes over, the ministry loses all focus. We need to encourage and utilize the desire for relationships, but it can't become the reason the ministry exists.

I want to mention one final component of college-age relationships that I never thought about until I'd been doing college ministry for a few years. I wondered why I felt like I was always starting over, like we just couldn't keep people involved long-term. I expected some turnover after four or five years, but I noticed that our core group was changing every two years. I couldn't figure out if we weren't engaging them or if they were just flaky. It turns out the problem wasn't me or the people involved. In fact, there really wasn't a problem at all, but a need for me to readjust my expectations of college-age people.

The first adjustment was to realize that some people wouldn't find what they needed in our ministry. No group can be all things to all people, and it's a waste of time to try. Some people feel weird if they show up and no one talks to them, while others feel weird if they spend the whole gathering in conversations with people they've just met. No formula ensures everyone will feel welcome and connected. So no matter what, there will always be people who show up for two or three gatherings and never come back. Sure, it's worth checking in with a phone call to see if they'd like to talk about something. But most of the time, I've found these people just don't have an interest in what we're doing.

The second adjustment was to realize that the lives of college-age people are very transient! In a group where some people are students, some are working full-time, some are doing nothing, and some are doing everything, college-age ministry has a fluidity that's unique from other age groups. Even the most committed people will have times when they can't be there, or they naturally lose desire to be involved. This transition can actually be a sign of health in the group. If people are moving on in life, then it means we're doing something right. Remember, the goal of college-age ministry is to help them move on.

My third adjustment involved recognizing just how emotional and stressful these years are for college-age people. The internal work they're doing as they search for identity and meaning and intimacy and truth can make them feel as though they live under constant pressure. And when people are under pressure, they tend to behave erratically. If some of the relationships they've formed in the group fall apart, they might leave. Often an outside issue with family or work stresses them out, and they need some time to work through whatever the problem is. Or they start dating someone who doesn't want to be part of the group. Or they need more money, so they have to work more. Or they aren't ready for the spiritual work the group involves, and they need to mature a little more.

Once I saw college-age people as they were—instead of how I thought they should be—I stopped worrying about the turnover. Naturally, I want people to stick with our ministry, but my focus needs to be on making sure the ministry is true to its mission, not making sure everyone is happy.

The relationships college-age people will develop in your ministry might become some of the most meaningful friendships in their lives. At this critical stage of development, strong Christian community and committed friends who know how to challenge and sharpen one another can be the very things that keep a college-age person engaged in the faith.

REDEFINING WORSHIP

College-age people love music. They're mature enough to tune in to the emotional quality of music, which makes listening to or creating music a rich experience for them. Music can also act as a bridge into spirituality. It's a safe way to express emotion and feel connected to others in the community. But the importance college-age people place on music means the quality of worship music can make or break a ministry experience. And that's a problem.

So often, I find that college-age people (and people of other ages, too) worship "worship." They believe the only way to really praise God is to sing certain kinds of songs and feel certain kinds of emotions. I'd guess that most of us agree worship is far more than singing songs (Romans 12:1-2). At the same time, churches typically refer to the musical part of a gathering time as "worship," leaving our college-age people with the impression that worship is only about singing. If we let them continue with that assumption, we rob them of a central element of their faith.

When we started our ministry, we didn't have anyone leading music on a consistent basis. Half the time we didn't have anyone at all. But as time went on, we started to develop a band. It was made up of people who had embraced the gospel, had a growing faith, wanted to serve, and had musical gifts. It was wonderful to have such a committed, talented group of people leading music. The problem was they got *really* good. I know that's a pretty nice "problem" to have, but this perceived success brought out some real issues.

Our band played a significant role in the rapid growth of our ministry. Our worship leader and I worked really well together, coordinating the music and the messages for each gathering time. We even wrote specific songs for some messages, making our gathering times seamless. The band practiced all the time; they were writing and recording, and people were really engaging with that part of our gatherings. Still, the worship leader and I recognized that people were engaging on an emotional level, but we weren't sure they were engaging with God. Thankfully, the band guys also understood the issue, and together we began to take significant steps to find a balance.

To get our group moving to a place where we could understand worship differently, I decided to teach through the book of 1 John. If you're familiar with this book, you know it's pretty straightforward—not many comforting thoughts in this one. I focused on how our relationship with God isn't solely based on our emotions. We also became intentional about the way we talked about worship. Our worship leader took time every week to talk about worship as a lifestyle and not as a four-song set. I encouraged our college-age people to think about worship as a life issue, not a "church" issue, by asking them what life looks like for someone who truly loves God.

We also began to implement other avenues of worship. We began to worship through prayer, public reading of Scripture, and fellowship. We created worship experiences that didn't involve any music at all. We planned one event that we promoted as a "worship night." People were so excited when they arrived, thinking it was going to be a big event of some kind. We held everyone outside the sanctuary until the last minute. When we finally let them in, the sanctuary was empty—no instruments, no setup, no chairs. It was pitch-black, and all you could see were large screens on which we projected these words, "Worship as long as you wish..." We didn't facilitate anything. We just let it be. Some people were confused, others left after a few minutes, but many stayed and spent time in prayer, read Scripture, or just sat quietly. It turned out to be the most worshipful experience we've ever "organized." It was also a pivotal point in our ministry and a great object lesson to help bring a balance.

At one point we went a step further—for four months we went without any musical expressions of worship. Yes, our attendance went down a bit, but most people loved it. They felt like it brought back the authenticity of our ministry. It was a refreshing time, a time in which a lot of growth took place in our people— and in me. Once we felt like we'd recalibrated, we slowly brought back the musical aspect of our gathering times.

As leaders, we need to consider not only the immediate needs of our people, but the long-term impact of what our ministry is teaching as well. We must think beyond what works and what brings in the numbers and focus on what guides college-age people toward maturity and deeper faith.

CREATING A SPACE

Our first organized gathering was a barbecue at my house. From there, we launched our Thursday-night gathering. We met in a classroom with no projector, no sound system, no candles, no special lighting, and, as I mentioned, sometimes no music at all. It didn't have any "atmosphere" whatsoever. It turns out the lack of ambience didn't matter.

I've spoken to countless people who want to start a college-age ministry and are trying to figure out how to go about it. So they visit ministry after ministry to see what others are doing. They take careful note of what elements they have in the gathering time, what decor they have, and so on. Then they go back to their churches, meet with a team of people, and talk about implementing what they found to be effective. Some will even buy lamps or candles or curtains to make the atmosphere similar to what they saw. But these ministries are bound to fail—or at least struggle to get going. You can't *start* a ministry where other ministries already *are*.

When people think about the word *atmosphere*, they're usually thinking about the physical elements in a room. Although I love to set up the lights in my living room in a certain way before I read late at night, and I know that lighting and art and music can have a tremendous impact on the feel of a worship experience, atmosphere is created by much more than physical elements. The atmosphere that matters most to college-age people will come from you, your ministry team, and the people involved in your group.

I understand what it's like to worry about last-minute details five minutes before an event starts, or to feel so rushed beforehand that I don't take a moment to pray for our time together. But I've learned that my mood at the start of a gathering can set the tone for the rest of the group. If I'm relaxed and relational when people arrive, they tend to be that way, too. You set the atmosphere by your attitude—whether it's rushed and program-oriented or relaxed and people-oriented.

College-age people *are* aware of the physical elements in a room, but they're more aware of the overall feel of the group. Physical elements can help you create a comfortable atmosphere, but all the dim lights in the world won't make up for closed-off people and tense leaders. If you want to put time and effort into creating an aesthetically pleasing meeting space, that's fine. But don't let the physical surroundings become what defines your ministry. Make sure relationships come first. Have places for people to sit and talk; add some food—food always helps people loosen up and feel comfortable; make sure your space is clean, but not so formal that people can't relax. Focus on the people, and the vibe will take care of itself.

Creating a gathering that meets the needs of college-age people is a lot less complicated than we might imagine. So instead of putting our energy into the big things, such as what kinds of events to plan and what kind of space to create, we leaders need to pay attention to the little things that truly matter to college-age people—the authenticity of the leadership, the attitudes of people, the sense that they're free to be who they are, the chance to build relationships. Create a gathering place where these elements are valued and encouraged, and you can have an effective ministry.

CHAPTER 11

THE VOLUNTEERS

Have you ever watched little kids play together? The other day I watched two kids—a boy and a girl—playing in the sand area at the park. I was sitting on the grass having a "picnic" with my daughter, Karis. (By "picnic" I mean a blanket laid on the grass and a ton of pretend food spread all around.) As Karis was preparing plates of "food" for lunch, I watched the other two kids digging in the sand. I try to give Karis my undivided attention when I'm with her, but you can eat only so many plastic apples before your mind starts to wander.

Anyway, as I watched the other two kids play, I was amazed at the differences between them. The girl was carefully creating a sand castle, while the boy was digging and throwing sand everywhere. The girl was talking to herself, singing in a soft little voice, and stopping now and then to watch other people at the park. The boy, on the other hand, wasn't making a sound except for an occasional grunt. He was digging aimlessly with a couple of sticks, and he was oblivious to everything and everyone around him.

Finally, the girl finished her sand castle. She stood up, took a bow (apparently I wasn't the only one watching), and raised her hands like a gymnast who just completed her floor routine. The boy looked over at her—and that's when he caught sight of the sand castle. With eyes locked on the target, arms flailing about, and legs rotating as fast as they could, he ran toward it. When he was about a foot away, the boy jumped and landed smack in the middle of her masterpiece. Then, just as the girl had done, he turned to the imaginary crowd and took a bow.

In his mind, sand castles were made for destroying—smashing it was a perfectly normal action to take. But the girl was absolutely bewildered by what he'd done. She stood there for a few seconds, staring at him in shock and silence. Then she laid into him. But the more she yelled, the more confused the boy looked. It was like he was thinking, *What is your problem? That was a lot of fun!*

To a spectator, this scene was very funny. But for the two kids involved, it was anything but. They found themselves stunned and confused by the other's actions.

I've seen the same thing happen in college-age ministries. A leader works and works and works to create a perfect ministry, only to have college-age people show up and find nothing of interest, leaving a "crushed" ministry behind them as they go. Both sides end up with nothing but shock and confusion.

We've already discussed some of the hallmarks of an effective college-age ministry, but an area that often gets glossed over during conversations about college-age ministry—and is therefore a lot like that sand castle waiting to be destroyed—is the use of volunteers. Those of us who come from a youth ministry background think we know just what we need to do to find and keep great volunteers. But what works in a youth setting can often be the very thing that sinks a college-age ministry.

BREAKING THE "TEAM" SPIRIT

One of the first steps I took when we started our college-age ministry gathering was getting together about 10 people who I thought would make a great leadership team. I wanted to have a core group of people who were committed to this ministry, had some gifts, wanted to serve, and last, but certainly not least, loved God. We started to meet before we launched the ministry, just to get to know each other better and jell as a group. We'd meet over coffee or pizza, talk about our ideas for the ministry, and think about our gifts and interests, eventually designating ministry areas for each person. It was a lot of fun and a wonderful start to what we were hoping to do.

As time went along, however, I found the "team" aspect got, well, weird. As important as teams are, they're also hard to keep motivated. Teams have a tendency to become stuck in their expectations about who does what. And they can quickly fall into a pattern of negativity. What started as heartfelt service eventually becomes duty.

We've all experienced this shift at one time or another. We get excited about being a part of something, but then it becomes a regular responsibility that we just *have* to get done. And once one team member gets in this rut, others will soon follow.

When our team hit this point, I started to think maybe I wasn't the person to lead this team—at least not the way I'd been leading it. I decided to give it another shot, so I revamped by bringing in a couple of fresh minds who definitely injected some new excitement into the team. We met biweekly for discussion, planning, and prayer. In some ways it felt like we were starting over again, but it seemed to help. But before long, we were in the same rut we'd been in before.

After failing at this leadership-team thing twice, I decided to give one of our ministry leaders a chance to put a team together. I handed the leadership over to him and let him run with it. He was much more gifted in small-group leadership than I am, and it seemed like a natural fit. He brought new people onto the team, and everyone was excited. I thought we'd finally hit on the solution, and then, once again, the energy died off. A fourth try with yet another leader ended the same way. The longest any of those teams stayed together and motivated was about four months—and that estimate might be a bit of an overstatement.

Not knowing what else to do, I dumped the idea of having any kind of leadership team at all. It was one of the best ministry decisions I've ever made.

College-age people are stimulated by change, adrenaline, emotions, relationships, and social activity. So a once-a-month meeting meant to delegate tasks quickly becomes boring—it's the ultimate "program-driven" experience. College-age people don't want a program, and they don't want to feel like they're only valuable because of what they can do for us. Leadership meetings feel like the worst combination of the two.

So rather than having a formal leadership team, I built a team of people who didn't know they were a team. I decided to focus on the relationships instead of the program. Not only was this reprioritization far more effective, but it also was much truer to who I am and where my strengths are. Instead of biweekly or monthly meetings with a team of people, I handpicked natural leaders and began meeting weekly with each of them. Adding eight or 10 meetings every week was obviously more work in some ways, but much less in others.

This approach certainly took more time, and collaborating schedules was always tough. But this new tactic completely changed our ministry for the better. Our time became about them, not about the programmatic tasks. Investing in them as individuals was much easier than trying to constantly motivate a team for accomplishing tasks. By simply moving my energy from team motivation to investing personally in those individuals, the tasks naturally took care of themselves.

I want to be clear here. I wasn't trying to trick these people into helping. I genuinely wanted to spend time with them as individuals. I wanted to know them better and help them find ways to live out who God had uniquely made them to be. If they didn't have the time or inclination to be involved in our ministry, I still would have enjoyed spending time with them.

I did, however, develop some "rules" for myself to make sure I didn't fall into the trap of using people:

- These meetings would be totally informal. We'd meet for coffee or lunch, or if I met with a female, we met at the picnic tables outside our church office.

- If I had ministry details to discuss, I'd remember them. I never brought a notepad or computer with me.

- I made sure the majority of the time was spent talking about the other person's life and personal thought processes.

- I tried as hard as I could to dig into their spiritual lives. When people serve faithfully, we tend to assume their faith is strong, but often the opposite is true.

- We'd laugh a lot.

- I'd talk about other ideas that had nothing to do with the ministry.

- I made sure they knew me and knew I loved them for who they were before I'd ever let them serve.

- I never asked them to do anything. I waited for them to let me know when they wanted to be more involved. And if they never asked, that was okay, too.

The real beauty of this approach was that I could have a personal relationship with each of them instead of having to act as a task delegator. We were partners in ministry, walking side by side with each other. We'd talk about what needed to be done in our ministry and work together to make it happen. It was a much better fit not only for me, but more importantly, for those with whom I was working.

About once a quarter I got all of these people together for a social gathering. We didn't discuss tasks, didn't walk through where the ministry was heading; we just hung out. After the very first time, they talked about getting together twice a month. They were happy to connect with others who were serving and wanted to develop those relationships. When it was required to meet twice a month, nobody wanted to. However, because the group was based on authentic relationships, not tasks, they wanted to connect more often. Eventually, meeting twice a month would have created the same problem all over again. So I encouraged them to stay connected outside of any formally organized event. And this arrangement was the key to making it work. Having a team that didn't know they were a team actually helped them view themselves as a team.

You might notice that I haven't said anything about the age of these volunteers. That's because I find that regardless of their age, people who are drawn to college-age ministry are drawn to relationships. While adult volunteers might not have the same transparent hunger for connections that college-age people have, those who have a passion for working with college-age people tend to share their desire for deep, meaningful connections. In other words, they don't like meetings either.

There are, however, some critical differences in the way a ministry leader inspires and works with volunteers of different ages and life stages. I've found that college-age peer leaders call for a somewhat different set of guidelines than their older counterparts. To help you create a ministry in which volunteers thrive right along with the rest of the group, it's essential to understand these differences.

PEER LEADERS

One of the best parts of college-age ministry is that it's fairly easy to find peer leaders. They're usually full of enthusiasm, energy, and great ideas. I love working with these young leaders and watching them discover how God uniquely made them to serve. At the same time, peer leadership is filled with potential problems that can run even the most well-intentioned ministry off its rails. To avoid these issues, I suggest these 11 guidelines for choosing and working with peer volunteers.

1. **Make sure they're ready to lead.** I've often failed to realize that the gifts of college-age people tend to far outweigh their maturity. The youth pastor with whom I interned saw gifts in me and sent me off into ministry, and I ended up with pride that was out of control. It wasn't his fault—he thought I could handle it. But few college-age people are as ready for leadership as we think they are. If we push them into leadership roles—or let them convince us they're ready for leadership—before they have the maturity to be leaders, we'll damage our ministries. Worse, we'll damage the hearts of these same young leaders we were hoping to nurture. Nothing kicks the foundation out from under a young

leader like exalting gift development over character. We want to support them with a long-term mindset, not destroy them with a short-term one. I believe that when we do what's best for the heart of the individual, we're doing what's best for the ministry.

2. **Check their motivations.** Experience has taught me to be wary of college-age volunteers who *really* want a position that gets them in front of people. Even if they're gifted speakers or musicians or organizers, the eagerness to be in a public role is a sign that they're more concerned about using their gifts than with growing in their faith. I know that statement sounds a little strange—we want them to use their gifts. But college-age people can get carried away with this desire, thinking they have to use their gifts in as public a way as possible for them to be really meaningful to God. Try to move these people into smaller roles where they can use—and nurture—their gifts in a balanced, protected way. If they reject that guidance, you automatically know they're not ready to lead. Our role is to foster spiritual health in our people, which sometimes means holding them back until their maturity catches up with their gifts and skills.

3. **Look for patterns of manipulation.** I'm not trying to say that we have to be suspicious of our college-age people. But we do have to remember what's going on inside of them during these years. Their primary motive is self-discovery. For some, that exploration means trying on various characteristics to see what feels right and what doesn't. Remember the Substitute personality from chapter 2, the one who changes his personality depending on the social atmosphere? Well, those Substitutes are great at figuring out who they need to be to fit into a ministry setting. They aren't necessarily morphing with malicious intent, but they do it just the same. The best way to avoid bringing this less-than-mature personality into leadership is to ask that your people be involved in the ministry for at least six months before taking on

any leadership responsibilities—and then start them slowly and with patience. You need time to see who they really are. And they need time to trust that they can be themselves.

4. **Ask the tough questions regarding pride and jealousy.** Late adolescents are becoming acutely aware of their own gifts, as well as the gifts of others. This awareness is a great help in identity formation, but it can also cause them to feel defeated when they see other people who are as good—or better—at doing something as they are. I've seen so many college-age people pursue leadership roles out of pride or envy, rather than out of a true desire to serve. I've also seen them fall into a kind of false humility—the kind they often learn from growing up in the church—that helps them avoid taking responsibility for their weaknesses and failures. The results are never healthy for them or for the ministry. This situation is another case where those one-on-one times pay off. I know the hearts of the people in leadership in our ministry because we've spent a lot of time talking, praying, and building a relationship. That investment allows me to have a fairly good sense of whether they struggle with issues like pride or jealousy. I'm able to help them become authentic, give them freedom to be honest about their failures, and then embrace them with grace when they do fail.

5. **Let them lead small groups, not Bible studies.** Even if you have college-age people who know their Bibles backward and forward, I believe people at this age stage can make lousy Bible study leaders. They might have strong convictions, but most still struggle with idealism and a somewhat shallow faith grounded in information, not well-thought-out belief. They become the blind leading the blind. I find college-age people do much better leading small, discussion-based groups where they're facilitators instead of teachers. But even then, I try to put only people I really know and trust in those roles.

6. Wait at least a year after someone becomes a believer before you put them into leadership. When college-age people become Christians, they tend to make radical changes in their lives. One of those changes is to jump into church life with a lot of enthusiasm. They want to contribute to something that has made such an impact on them. But they have to learn to be a part of the body before they can lead the body. When we place new Christians in leadership too soon, we can give them a false sense of identity in which they don't have time to just be a Christian. Part of discipling new Christians is giving them time to explore and embrace their new faith in everyday life without feeling like they have to have all the answers.

7. Be patient with their disorganization. College-age people typically struggle with discipline and organization—remember that feeling? Working with college-age volunteer leaders will often test our patience, but our role is to give them the right combination of guidance and freedom. I shoot for a kind of relaxed formality where I'm clear about what I expect from them, but gracious when they forget a detail or lose focus. Again, having a relationship makes all the difference in these circumstances. In my weekly conversations with my college-age volunteers, we talk about issues such as what they see as their weaknesses. I find most college-age people already know they have a hard time with discipline, and they're usually eager for some help in growing up in this area. So when a detail slips or they don't follow through on a commitment, we can talk about it as a life issue, not a ministry problem.

8. Pay attention to dating relationships. Lots of dating relationships start and end in college ministry. They can add either strength and joy to a group, or drama and destruction—especially when one or both of the people involved are in leadership. Because college-age people are socially motivated, these types

of situations can cause major tension in networks of friends and have a ripple effect on the whole ministry. As leaders, we need to keep an eye on dating relationships and intervene when we see problems—or even potential problems. At the same time, our motivation always needs to be a desire to do what's best for the people involved, knowing that what's best for them will be what's best for the ministry as well.

We had a situation where two people who were dating planned to go on the same mission trip. In December, when we picked our teams for the July trip, they'd been dating for a few months. Everything was going well, so they thought it would be great to be on the same team. But I wasn't convinced. So instead, I moved one of them to a different team, one that would be serving two weeks earlier than the other. The timing meant that between the two trips, they wouldn't see each other for a month.

You might think I'm cruel (they certainly did), but a month after we purchased our plane tickets, they broke up. If they'd been on the same trip, it could've been a major disruption for the rest of the team. Even if they'd stayed together, that time spent apart could've been very beneficial. It was an unpopular decision on my part, but I believe it was in everyone's best interest.

9. Invest in the whole person. I've talked a lot about building relationships with college-age people so we're able to guide them toward maturity. But these relationships can't just be about helping them. We need to do with them what we do with our friends: Laugh a lot, talk about nothing, share what's going on in our lives, and offer advice when we're asked for it, but don't play the role of therapist. Just be present and show them we're truly interested in who they are.

10. Allow them to lead. This advice might sound rather obvious, but I've seen far too many college-age people get burned

out on leadership because the pastor or ministry leader never gives them real responsibility. Trust is a major issue for college-age people. They want to know their ideas and input are taken seriously. They want to take an assignment and show you they can complete it. As I said earlier, sometimes they'll flake out on you, but we have to use those times as opportunities to help them grow, not excuses to withhold our trust.

11. Be on the lookout for potential leaders. We tend to wait for leaders to rise up, rather than raising them up ourselves. Most leadership positions in a college ministry will have about a two-year turnover rate. A few people will be around longer, but many will have moved on, and others will have moved in. Pay attention to the recent high school grads coming in to your ministry. They'll have fresh energy and enthusiasm for what you're doing. I'm not saying you should put them in leadership before they're ready. Instead, put effort into getting to know them.

We can easily fall into a pattern of overseeing all the details of ministry, but ignoring people's hearts and souls. Hebrews 13:17 says, "Have confidence in your leaders and submit to their authority, because they keep watch over you as those who must give an account. Do this so that their work will be a joy, not a burden, for that would be of no benefit to you." We're accountable for how we guide people toward spiritual maturity. That fact is as true with our college-age leaders as it is with everyone else in our ministry.

"OLDER" LEADERS

Adult volunteers are an important part of any student ministry, but they're absolutely vital to college-age ministry. If the goal is to assimilate students into the adult life of the church, then we must expose them to older adults. Thankfully, college-age people long to have older adults in their lives. They have great respect for older people—the older, the better! Ironically, they especially appreciate knowing people their parents' age, just not their parents. I find that they value the opinions, advice, and experience of these older adults because they come without the presumed bias that their parents bring to the relationship.

I learned very quickly that these relationships are so special to college-age people that the worst thing I could do was refer to the older volunteers as "staff." The college-age people wanted to have genuine friendships with these older adults, and to call them *staff* made it feel like a business relationship, not a friendship.

So instead of bringing older adults "on staff," I simply make introductions. Our adult volunteers are people whom I've gotten to know and love and who just happen to have a heart for college-age people. Sometimes I make a one-on-one introduction when I know a college-age person who'd really click with one of these older adults. Other times I invite them to the group and introduce them as one of my friends whom I respect. Then I let the personal connections happen on their own.

As great as older adult volunteers can be, I'm pretty picky about the kind of volunteer I want to join our ministry. Even those with the best intentions can have a detrimental effect on the group if they're there to "fix" the college-age people, or if they're easily frustrated with the inconsistency and lack of discipline in college-age people. I use a mental checklist when I think about adult volunteers. I believe it provides a good perspective on what you need to look for in older volunteers:

1. **They have an authentic faith.** These volunteers are role models for what I hope to see develop in our college-age people. So I want them to be people who don't just profess the faith, but who also integrate it into every aspect of their lives.

2. **They defy categories.** I don't care if our adult volunteers are business owners or stay-at-home moms, introverts or extroverts, single or married, musicians or engineers, loaded or broke—the more variety, the better. Not only does a wide array of people increase the chances that our college-age people will find someone with whom to connect, but it also reinforces the idea that what you do and what you have doesn't define who you are.

3. **Married couples that have solid marriages.** There's something really wonderful about having married couples involved in college-age ministry. College-age people have high hopes of being married one day, but many have never been around healthy families. Volunteers who have a solid, godly marriage can be excellent examples for college-age people who are in the midst of developing their sense of identity and their understanding of what intimacy looks like. Exposing late adolescents to people with godly characteristics indirectly but appropriately guides the differentiation and integration process we talked about earlier.

4. **They're highly relational.** I expect our adult volunteers to have coffee with our college-age people. I expect them to care and know how to build a friendship. So I expect them to be people who thrive on relationships. They don't have to be out-there extroverts. In fact, some of the most effective volunteers are introverts who love building deep connections. I also expect them to have a heart for college-age people. Before older people become volunteers, I spend a lot of time telling them what to expect. And even before they ask to get involved, I pick out people I think would be a great addition to our ministry and start talking about

what we do and what's going on in the lives of our college-age people. I try to lay the groundwork for the relationships I expect to form.

5. **They're biblically grounded.** My hope is that our older volunteers carry out our mission to help college-age people mature in their faith. To achieve this mission, they have to have a solid grasp of the Bible. They don't need seminary degrees—just the spiritual maturity to guide college-age people through the process of developing a deeper faith. They need to understand the teaching and discipleship approach I discussed in chapter 9 and be willing to take college-age people into the deeper levels of thought that are needed at this stage.

I realize this list can be rather daunting—especially when you're desperate to find any volunteers, much less those who meet all of these expectations. But these people are in your church. They might not stand out as the cool people or the obvious choices to work with college-age people. However, I promise you, there are adults in your church who have the potential to be great assets to your ministry.

Perhaps the biggest difference between peer leaders and older leaders is the amount of time they should put into the ministry. And even though I've just been talking about how great those older volunteers can be, I think we need to limit their involvement.

I know that suggestion sounds strange, so let me explain. College-age people crave help finding direction in their lives and have all kinds of questions they'd like to ask older adults, but they also want the space and freedom to figure things out themselves. They want to have someone to talk to, but not all the time. They don't mind having a mentor, but they don't want another parent.

Having adults on hand at specific times can be a tremendous attraction for college-age people, but having them around too much can change the atmosphere of your ministry.

What it boils down to isn't the number of adult volunteers or their age or their passion. It's their presence. If they're involved in the weekly planning meetings and are working at every gathering, they're viewed as staff. Suddenly these great friends feel like chaperones. And no college-age person wants a chaperone.

Instead, think of your older volunteers as waiting in the wings. The majority of adults involved in our ministry have never attended one of our weekly gatherings. They're people I've come to know and love and have asked if they'd be willing to walk alongside our younger people. When I meet a college-age person who wants to be mentored, I connect them with one of my older adult friends.

My family and I often have small groups of eight to ten college-age people join us at our house for dinner. When we do, I invite one or two older adults to join us as well. The dinner doesn't have any agenda, so the presence of these older people has no agenda, either. They're just there to hang out and laugh with us. I also try to have two or three couples join us on weekend retreats. I shoot for one couple for every 15 college-age people to keep the balance about right. This approach provides plenty of natural, casual chances for our college-age people to get to know these older mentors.

There are all kinds of handbooks to help you manage your volunteers effectively. My advice is to avoid them at all costs. When it comes to college-age ministry, there isn't a model for what a great volunteer looks like because the whole point is relationships, and relationships simply can't be planned out.

Instead, be flexible, make sure your volunteers know what you expect of them, and then get out of the way while they connect with the other people in your ministry. That approach is what leadership looks like in college-age ministry.

CHAPTER 12

THE ASSIMILATION

I recently spoke at a conference and had the privilege of meeting Gary, the pastor of a small church in Illinois. We started talking after one of my seminars and ended up having lunch together. After sitting down with him for five minutes, I absolutely loved this guy. He told me his church was struggling to hold on to their young people when they graduated from high school. Many of the families in his church had experienced their children disconnecting from the church after high school, and they were brokenhearted about it. Gary was meeting with parents, praying with them, and walking alongside them in their pain and fear. Gary felt that fear himself—his daughter was about to graduate from high school, and he didn't want to see the same thing happen to her.

Gary's heart for the people in his church was unbelievable. His concern for these families—the parents and the kids—kept him up at night. He was looking for some advice on how to keep college-age people engaged in the life of the church.

It didn't take me long to figure out what the problem was. Gary certainly had a deep love for his people, and he had great ideas for ministry. The problem was that everything they'd tried in their church involved getting these college-age people to attend a church service or other big event—and by now you know why that approach didn't cut it.

On top of that, these kids grew up calling the church service "big church" and never felt like they belonged there. Even after they graduated, big church felt like something meant for "real" adults, not late adolescents. The messages were about adult and family life. Every sermon illustration had to do with the workplace or parenting. The life of the church revolved around people they didn't know or thought of as their parents' friends and their friends' parents. It just didn't connect with where they were in life. Gary and others tried to get the kids involved in various service projects and ministries—working in the church nursery, helping with Sunday school, that kind of thing. But nothing seemed to keep these young people interested.

Gary had fallen into the trap of believing that assimilation was about connecting college-age people to a church service. The tradition of Christian life revolving around the church service drastically affected Gary's idea of what it meant to assimilate high school graduates. His motivation was right, but his methods couldn't have been more wrong.

The goal of assimilation is to have college-age people become fully integrated into adult relationships apart from the church service or organized events. And in this case, it had to start with Gary. I'm sure he was a fine pastor, but college-age people don't care about a person's role. The young people at Gary's church knew who he was and what position he held, but they had no clue how much he loved them. Gary's compassion was his greatest strength, and they didn't even know it!

Gary went home after the seminar and began looking for a leader with a heart for college-age people. Within a couple of weeks, the church hired a part-time person. Gary and I talked during this process, and I encouraged him to make sure his leader focused on relationships, not programs. I also encouraged him to let the parents of the college-age people know that they'd all need to change their assumptions about what engagement with the church would look like for their children. Assimilation would take time, and it would take a whole new set of practices for this church.

The same might be true in your setting. You've inherited assumptions and ideas about how to assimilate college-age people back into the church, ideas that simply haven't worked. But the real issue is that so many college-age ministries have the wrong understanding of "assimilation." When I speak to leaders of college-age ministries, I ask them to define the goal of their ministry. So often, the answer involves assimilating college-age people into the life of the church by getting them to serve their faith community and finding ways to help them feel more comfortable in the church service. If that's the goal, then not only will a ministry fail miserably, but it might also reinforce the disconnection between college-age people and the church.

I know pastors and leaders have nothing but the best intentions when they try to make their church services more "user-friendly" for college-age people. But even the best speakers and bands and lighting equipment won't make a college-age person come to something that isn't hitting their life issues and core need for relationships—mentor and peer. I used to serve at a church where the pastor, Francis Chan, was one of the top youth speakers in the world. That assertion is *not* an overstatement! Francis can absolutely communicate with people no matter how old they are. But even in that context, with Francis as our pastor, our ministry had to go beyond getting people to show up for church. If I couldn't do it with that approach and with a pastor like Francis, then my hunch is that you can't do it either.

Thinking about ministry outside of the program and event models—and I consider a church service to be an event—is tough for us. Yet that thinking is exactly what we need to have if we're going to act as a bridge for college-age people to enter the life of the church.

In my years of working in college-age ministry, I've found seven focus areas that are essential for real assimilation to take place. They're the keys to helping college-age people cultivate a positive attitude toward being part of a Christian community. They don't cost anything. They don't demand a big staff or even a big ministry. Any church, in any context, can use this list to move college-age people into active engagement with the body of Christ.

REDEFINING CHURCH

Most of us would agree that church is the people, not the buildings. But do our ministries reflect that belief? When we talk about connecting people to the church, what do we mean? As leaders, we get frustrated by the consumer mentality so pervasive in churches. But the truth is, we create it. Think about the way you describe your ministry or your church. When most people talk about their churches, they talk about the programs they offer, the services they provide. The underlying message is that we have a product to promote, and we need to sell it with as many bells and whistles as possible.

If we want college-age people to engage in the life of the church, then we have to change the way we talk about church. The church is people—people of all ages—not programs or buildings (1 Peter 2:4-10). The church is made up of the children of God who seek to imitate him in every way (Ephesians 5:1). The church is about people seeking reconciliation with God (Ephesians 2:11-22) and with one another (Ephesians 4:3).

When we define church by the programs we offer, involvement means little more than moving from one kind of event to another, from one youth room to a different youth room. College-age people need—and want—so much more. They want to be a part of something meaningful, something real, something lasting. They want to be part of the church.

IGNORING THE NUMBERS

I know some people read what I say about programs and events and think, *What about the large ministries with bands, lights, video clips, and great speakers? Some of these ministries have hundreds of college-age people coming to them. You can't say what they're doing isn't effective!*

Actually, I can. I'm going to try to be tactful here, but the reality is, I get pretty fired up about this subject. I find people tend to agree with me that programs shouldn't be our focus—in theory. But walking through the implications of that statement is where the rubber meets the road. Having numerical attendance as the measure of effectiveness goes right back to the message that the church is its programs. But in fact, when our ministry was at its highest attendance, we were also the least effective.

While it's true that healthy, effective ministries tend to grow rather than die out, I don't believe numerical growth is the best measure of effectiveness. The "if a few is good, then more must be better" mentality isn't biblical; it's cultural. It's a purely American way of thinking. And it's repulsive to college-age people. They feel like a commodity, a body in a seat. More than anything, they want to matter, to have a sense of identity and purpose. Focusing on numbers tells them they're just that—a number. It's a mentality that chips away at the very heart of college-age ministry.

LEADING THROUGH SERVICE

Service is one of the hallmarks of college-age ministry—but not the kind of service that might come to your mind. Instead of trying to plug college-age people into the church by having them serve, leaders need to focus on serving college-age people. In so many ways, college-age people are the "poor in spirit." They're stressed out, lonely, uncertain, and searching for a sense of who they are and what their lives might mean. They need people to care about all of those issues.

Serving college-age people is all about showing them we care. We do that by being available when they want to talk; by inviting them out for coffee just to check in; by taking an active, genuine interest in their lives. Walking with and shepherding people is what church leadership is about. There will come a time when college-age people want to serve others, but they need to make that choice themselves. We can't make it for them.

FOSTERING UNITY

A sense of connection and unity—especially cross-generational unity—is crucial for assimilation. A college-age ministry can never feel like an island unto itself. As leaders, we need to keep talking about the ways our ministry flows into the lives of others in the church and vice versa. We need to make those connections as reminders to our college-age people, but we also need to make them as reminders to other church staff.

You might not be in a position to influence the way other leaders handle their ministries, but you can certainly advocate for yours. Keep pressing the message that all people—from the youngest children to the oldest adults—need to feel like they're an essential part of the church. Every age group has an important role in the life of a church, and it's the leaders' job to make sure people know what their roles are.

Instead of always separating people by their differences, churches need to celebrate the unity they have as believers. Concepts like "big church" only serve to divide people and imply that some age groups are more valuable than others. Even if you can't do much about the overall structure of your church, you can remind other leaders of the important role your ministry plays in the life of the church.

You can also help build a sense of unity by encouraging continuity between various age-stage ministries. The ministry leaders on your church staff need to see themselves as being a part of something bigger, as being on a team, as handing off the people in whom they've invested to other leaders they trust. You can help develop this sensibility in your staff by including them in your ministry in various ways.

In our ministry, I invite other staff to spend time with us now and then. I try to expose the strengths of these staffers, so those who are great teachers are invited to teach, those with great ideas come in for a Q&A time, those who are just really wonderful people to know are included in one of the dinners at my house. They're always encouraged to take a college-age person out for coffee or join us on a retreat. They don't have to offer any leadership, just friendship and one more avenue for our people to connect with the life of the church.

Bringing the other staff into our ministry allows college-age people to see and get to know the hearts of others in the church. That exposure gives them a better sense of the deeper mission of the church itself, making it far more natural for them to integrate into the life of the community. It also allows the church staff to see and understand the growth, passion, and desire in our college-age people. Once they do, I find the staff starts reaching out in very personal, intentional ways. And when that outreach happens, assimilation is sure to follow.

CULTIVATING MENTORSHIPS

In chapter 11, I talked about the important role older adult volunteers play in a college-age ministry. But college-age people also need to have mentoring relationships with older people. In some ways, being a mentor is very much a part of what it means to volunteer in our college-age ministry. But some older adults balk at the idea of volunteering—it sounds like they're going to be stuck setting up chairs for the next five years. Mentorship allows older adults to connect with college-age people in a much more personal way, creating the kinds of connections that lead to assimilation.

Mentorship doesn't have to be a formal setup. I find the most effective mentoring happens when college-age people don't realize they're being mentored. Every year our church holds a men's houseboat retreat, and I usually try to get a group of college-age guys to attend. The plan is for guys to ride wakeboards and Jet Skis and just hang out for a long weekend. Each boat is given a certain amount of food, and the captain is responsible for making sure the meals are cooked for the entire crew. This year I made sure the college-age guys' boat was short on food and docked next to a boat full of older guys whom I knew would make great mentors. I worked with the captain of this older guys' boat to let him know what I was up to. We stocked his boat with extra food, knowing the hungry college-age guys next door would float over for some snacks before too long. Sure enough, on the very first afternoon, the men offered their extra food to the younger guys and even offered to cook it for them!

This strategy was extremely effective and was a major catalyst to building natural relationships. There's a fine line between leadership and manipulation, but in this case, it worked—and worked well! The point is to do our best at putting people in proximity to one another and praying that relationships happen naturally.

FOCUSING ON THE NEW KIDS

If you really want your college-age people to flow back into the life of the church, you have to know when to kick them out. This idea might go against everything you believe about ministry, but it's just one more way college-age ministry flips conventional wisdom upside down.

In most ministry models, you want to build relationships early on and keep strengthening those relationships over time. It's very easy to begin a ministry with new high school graduates, get close to them, and stay focused on them as they get older. The problem is, you'll end up alienating future high school graduates. Assimilation isn't just about moving college-age people back into the church; it's about keeping high school graduates engaged in the first place. If a college-age ministry drifts toward the needs of those on the older end of the age range, it will lose those on the younger end. And if the young end doesn't get involved, pretty soon there is no older end.

Focusing on the younger college-age people also allows those in their 20s to feel older—a necessary component of assimilation. If they don't eventually feel too old for the college-age group, then assimilation is going to be very difficult. We want our older college-age people to see where they've come from, to know that they aren't there anymore, and to want to take the next step that leads them more fully into the life of the church.

This element of assimilation, however, won't work unless we've focused on the other elements as well. If someone begins to feel old but we haven't done our job by connecting her to older believers, then the only thing we've done is prolong her sense of detachment. If a college-age person leaves our ministry while still having no sense of belonging or of being a vital part of the church, then we've left her in worse shape than when we found her.

BELIEVING IN YOUR MINISTRY

So many of the college-age-ministry leaders I talk to have the same frustration—they just aren't attracting many people. Even if low attendance doesn't bother them, they often work with a senior pastor or answer to a board of elders who wants to see numbers. I know it can be discouraging to put so much time and passion into something, only to have 10 people to show for it. But as I've said so often in this book, college-age ministry can't be about numbers. It has to be about people.

If you take nothing else away from this book, then I hope to have driven this point home. Don't worry about how you're going to get more people to come to an event or gathering; just spend one-on-one time with those who are there. If the people in authority over you don't understand that focus, give them this book. If you continue to face pressure to get high numbers of people to a weekly event, then leave that church and continue discipling the people with whom you're connected. I'm not kidding. Leave. You'll never be able to accomplish what you need to in that context. And if you give up and try to develop a program-based ministry, it will ultimately fail anyway.

I don't know how we got to the point where the number of people coming to an event determines whether or not a ministry is successful. Did you know that most scholars say the church at Thessalonica was likely made up of about 50 people? Yet look at what Paul says about that church:

> We always thank God for all of you and continually mention you in our prayers. We remember before our God and Father your work produced by faith, your labor prompted by love, and your endurance inspired by hope in our Lord Jesus Christ.
>
> For we know, brothers and sisters loved by God, that he has chosen you, because our gospel came to you not simply with words but also with power, with the Holy Spirit and deep conviction. You know how we lived among you for your sake. You became imitators of us and of the Lord, for you welcomed the message in the midst of severe suffering with the joy given by the Holy Spirit. And so you became a model to all the believers in Macedonia and Achaia. The Lord's message rang out from you not only in Macedonia and Achaia—your faith in God has become known everywhere.
> (1 Thessalonians 1:2-8)

Paul praises the deep faith of this church, but from an American perspective, we wouldn't give this church the time of day. We certainly wouldn't invite the pastor to speak at our conferences or buy his books. He'd be considered a failure for his tiny congregation.

If we're going to engage and assimilate college-age people into the life of our churches, we must focus on them as individuals. They aren't numbers or potential "giving units"; they're our brothers and sisters in Christ. When we spend time guiding college-age people toward spiritually mature conclusions on issues such as identity, intimacy, meaning, pleasure, and truth, then we've done our job. If they never come to an event, that's all right. If the only "formal" ministry you have is inviting a few college-age people over for dinner once a week, you're still being faithful. You don't need to *do* more. Just keep walking alongside college-age people and investing in their faith. If you stay focused on this mission, you'll see them through their post-high school years—one of the most challenging, altering, extraordinary stages of life.

Appendices

WORKING ON A COMMUTER CAMPUS

Reaching people on a commuter campus can be a daunting and discouraging venture. Students tend to be there strictly for the classes, and they don't hang around. Most of them have jobs. Some of them have families. This lack of a campus community makes meeting people and building relationships with students totally time-consuming. The lack of community also means these students are often the most detached college-age people. But there are ways we can be effective ministers to students on commuter campuses. Here are seven ideas:

1. **Impact one student at a time.** It's the best way to build community on a commuter campus. During your time with your students, spend a great deal of time cultivating in them a heart for their peers at school. Help them view their school as the mission field in which they're uniquely suited to serve.

2. **Limit events to half an hour.** Students are typically on the go and don't have a desire to be involved with on-campus events. Hosting a short lunchtime Bible study or getting

people connected for a morning "coffee break" can help them get to know others without feeling pressed for time.

3. **Consider serving the students.** Hand out coffee and hot chocolate on cold days, or cold soda and water on hot ones. Clean the windshields of people's cars while they're in class and leave a note under the wiper explaining why you did it. Hand out coffee during finals week. These little acts of kindness are a great way to catch the attention of busy students.

4. **Take a class.** Auditing a class might seem weird at first, but it can be a great way of getting to know some students on campus. Most commuter schools have a lot of older people attending anyway, so you don't have to worry about standing out. Philosophy or general religion classes are a great place to start. Schools typically have a class titled something like, "Man, Nature, God." These classes are often discussion-oriented and can be a great way to make contact with students who are searching for some spiritual connections. And you never know—you might learn something, too!

5. **Connect with the philosophy teachers.** Many of these professors will ask guests from different belief systems to come talk about a particular issue in class and may extend that invitation to you. While you shouldn't use this time to recruit people to your ministry, you can let the students know you're someone who's interested in exploring faith and thought in deeper ways. If they're interested in what you have to say, they'll ask about how they can learn more.

6. **Start a club.** I wouldn't recommend starting a "Christian" club—Christian groups tend to have a real stigma about

them. But starting a club to discuss social justice, human trafficking, or community service can be an effective way of meeting people who are eager to engage with these issues from a faith perspective.

7. **Get to know the facilities staff.** They have keys to everything! These contacts can really pay off for you when you need access to a meeting space or a quiet corner for prayer.

WORKING IN A COLLEGE TOWN

Doing ministry in a context where a major university is nearby brings lots of wonderful opportunities, but it also brings some serious challenges. The biggest challenge is the sense of competition between the local church and the campus-ministry organizations. To me, this false competition boils down to both parties having a program-driven philosophy of ministry. When everyone's out to build his own program, there's bound to be competition. If we stay focused on discipleship and assimilation, however, there's no reason why our churches can't complement the work of all those campus ministries.

The best way to put an end to the sense of competition is by serving *in* those campus ministries. Rather than duplicating efforts, it makes more sense to join forces, come alongside each other, and support each other with our resources. Here are eight ways you can help bridge the chasm between local churches and campus ministries so both of you can do more to reach out to college-age people:

1. **Search your own heart.** Work through any bitterness or competition you've been feeling. You don't have to agree with everything a particular ministry does, but at the very least, you must be the person who seeks unity with campus ministries. If you can't get past personal competitiveness, bitterness, or judgment, you don't need to read any further or try to bridge the gap. You won't get anywhere if you start with mixed motivations.

2. **Meet regularly with the campus-ministry leader.** Have coffee or lunch together so you can build a genuine relationship. Ask her how you can pray for the ministry. Offer your support and ask nothing in return. Most of all, mean it.

3. **Offer your church facilities.** Let them know they're welcome to use your church spaces—free of charge—for anything they need or want to do. Providing services to them will help break down any walls they may have. Yes, this suggestion also exposes college-age people to what's going on in your church, but that exposure can't be your motivation. This invitation is about serving the campus ministry, not building yours.

4. **If possible, offer to help a ministry financially.** You may even want to designate a portion of your own budget (if you have one!) toward a campus ministry. Personal fundraising alone supports most of these ministries, so a little help sponsoring an event is always appreciated. If they're holding a car wash or other fundraiser, go help them. These small gestures go a long way toward building trust and unity.

5. **Seek the leader's advice for your ministry.** Chances are, they have great insights into life on campus and the struggles college students are facing. They've likely developed a

great ministry philosophy that meets these needs. There's no reason to compete when it comes to serving college-age people. They need all the care and guidance they can get.

6. **Join forces on outreach events.** Come alongside another ministry, serving them in any way you can. Whether it's putting up posters, handing out flyers, being a part of planning meetings, loaning them a portable sound system, or simply letting them use your church copy machine, extra hands and minds are always welcome.

7. **Connect older people in your church with the campus ministry.** Showing students the benefits of having older believers in their lives can help them connect to a local church. Even if they don't connect to your church, it's likely that you'll have provided an experience that will make them feel more comfortable wherever they do connect. Your role can be exposing them to the church body, to life beyond their campus. In my mind, that's a phenomenal ministry!

8. **Consider mentoring a campus-ministry leader.** Many of these ministries have staff who are right out of college themselves and who might appreciate learning from your experience. Once you've established a trusting relationship with the ministry leader, ask your friend if a mentoring relationship would be helpful—and if it would be, make it happen.

"ALL MY STUDENTS GO AWAY TO COLLEGE"

I know a number of youth pastors who are interested in college-age ministry but have no college-age people to whom they can minister. They tell me all of their high school students leave town after graduation, leaving these pastors unsure of how to stay connected. Here are 10 strategies I've found to be effective in continuing a ministry to out-of-town students:

1. **Go on a campus visit with your high school students.** You can go with them on a scouting trip or when they move. Either way, it shows you're not dropping them. Instead, you're excited about their next stage of life, want to be a part of it, and will be there to support them. Trust me, this involvement will keep the door open for a relationship. It could even be worth assigning part of your budget (if you have one) to the cost of traveling. While you're on campus, meet with some local pastors to find out what kind of support they offer college students. Then let your student know what options are available for church participation.

2. **Pick up the phone.** If you're not able to go to the campus, set up phone appointments with the student or with college-ministry pastors at churches in the area. Talk to them about their philosophy of ministry, how they see incoming freshmen fitting into their church, and so on. Building this type of relationship lays the groundwork for your student. After getting to know the pastor and possibly listening to some podcasts, you may be able to recommend a church to your student. Then follow up to see how things are going and whether or not a connection is happening. Having you help and walk alongside them in this process will mean more to them than you realize.

3. **Develop a Facebook group strictly for graduates from your church.** Make this group invite-only. This way you can post blogs, send messages, and keep up on what's going on in the lives of your graduates. This social-networking group can also be a way for your students to stay in contact with each other. You can even schedule casual events during the holidays when they're back in town and use the Facebook group to get everyone involved.

4. **Pay attention to important times in their school year—particularly finals week.** Make sure you call your students during this time to let them know you're praying for them. If you can, send care packages with movie coupons or gift certificates to a local coffee shop. It's a small gesture that will mean a lot.

5. **Send care packages from the whole church.** It's one thing for you to mail a package, but it's something else for students to get a care package from their church family. Sending rolls of quarters for laundry, laundry soap, or gift certificates to fast-food restaurants can go a long way toward making sure these students know they're still loved and remembered.

6. **Host a blog for graduates.** You can write up posts on what you've been thinking about, recap the messages from the services in your church, update them on what's happening back home, or even have a few students rotate the blogging responsibilities. One of the most effective blog elements we've come up with is to have older believers from the church post messages from time to time. They write about the ways they've been praying for our college students and might even share a few stories about their own college days. Regardless of how you use the blog, it's a great interactive point of connection.

7. **Host an informal gathering during the holidays.** Just having an ice-skating party or hosting a barbecue at someone's house is enough. Don't make up invitations or plan a big event. Keep it low-key so people get the chance to reconnect.

8. **Point them to www.LiveAbove.com.** This ministry deals with more than 4,000 campuses and more than 1,000 military bases. They've compiled a database of high school grads from all over the world who are attending a college and want to connect with a local church. College ministries (or churches in general) can register as well and get the contact information of freshmen coming to their area. Once your students find a church, do a little homework so you know what kind of church it is. If you have concerns, share them, but I've found this site to be a great tool for students who want to find a church while they're at college.

9. **Help them get involved with a campus ministry.** Christian groups on campus are a good way to make sure they have an immediate avenue for connecting with others. If they don't connect soon after getting to school, they may never do so. Call the person who heads up the ministry and make

a point to let that person know you've got students coming to the school. Let your students know you care enough about them to make sure they get involved. If you can, get the ministry leader and your students connected through email, phone, an online network, or in person.

10. **Call, text, or email often and randomly.** Better yet, ask other people to do the same. Invite a few people who know the student to check in and ask how they can pray for your student in a particular week. Just knowing someone is thinking about them can really be an encouragement to college students who are living away from home.

It's important to remember that most of this stuff doesn't take a lot of our time, but it does go a long way in our relationships with the students who move away. Nearly every college student deals with a sense of loneliness and detachment. Your occasional call, text, or package—not to mention your efforts to help them get connected with ministries on campus—will let them know they're not alone and there's someone out there who loves them.

USING THIS BOOK AT A LEADERSHIP RETREAT

Hopefully, you've gotten to the end of this book with your head full of questions and thoughts about your college-age ministry. I encourage you to use the ideas you've read here as a starting point for your next leadership retreat. Really dig in to the theology and ideology behind what you've been doing and what you hope to do from here on out. You can utilize this book in a number of ways, but here are 10 suggestions to get you started:

1. **Talk about the reasons college-age people become detached and disengaged from the church.** What factors are at play in your church? As a team, talk about ways your ministry can address those factors. What hurdles might stand in your way? How can you move past those hurdles as a team?

2. **Think about what assimilation means to you.** Why is it an essential goal in college-age ministry? List practical ways your ministry can be focused on this goal. You might need to rework a lot of what you're doing to make assimilation possible. Make sure you talk through aspects of your mindset or ministry that might be undermining true assimilation.

3. **Walk through the different stages of identity formation discussed in chapter 2.** Using a whiteboard, list the five types: SUBSTITUTE, FLOATER, EXPLORER, TENTMAKER, THEOLOGIAN. Discuss each stage and then list the people in your ministry and where they might be in regard to these stages. Pray specifically for them and talk about how you can help each individual work toward being the Theologian.

4. **Talk about the college-age person's search for meaning.** Discuss the healthy and unhealthy parts of this process. Then think about the people in your ministry. Where are they finding meaning? What can you be doing in your ministry to help them find meaning in their relationships with God?

5. **Discuss how the pursuit of pleasure is impacting your ministry.** Are there ways your ministry is unintentionally reinforcing selfishness in your college-age people? How can you encourage discipline and self-control through your relationships with college-age people?

6. **Talk about what leadership looks like for college-age people.** What do they need from your team? What can they teach your team? Talk through any tensions you're dealing with as a group. College-age people can spot conflict a mile away, and they need to see how you deal with it.

7. **Determine if your ministry is program-driven or relationship-driven.** Think through your answers to this one because we often convince ourselves that our programs are all about people, when really, they're about numbers. Discuss your motivation as leaders—are you focused on the people or the task? Encourage your team to be honest with each other by being honest about your motivations as well. If it's tasks, figure out ways you can be more intentionally focused on the people.

8. **Look at what kind of teaching you've been doing.** Are you falling into the legalism of the law, or are you bringing your college-age people into a better understanding of grace? Think through the issues raised in chapter 9. What assumptions are underlying your teaching? How can you help your college-age people start moving into deeper thinking about their faith?

9. **Spend time talking through chapter 11.** Give your team the chance to share their experiences as volunteers. What's working? What isn't? What does your team need to stay motivated and focused on ministry?

10. **Compile a list of older people in your church who'd make great mentors for college-age people.** What can you do to get these people connected with college-age people? Then spend time talking about how your ministry will define "assimilation." What will it look like to successfully assimilate college-age people into the life of the church?

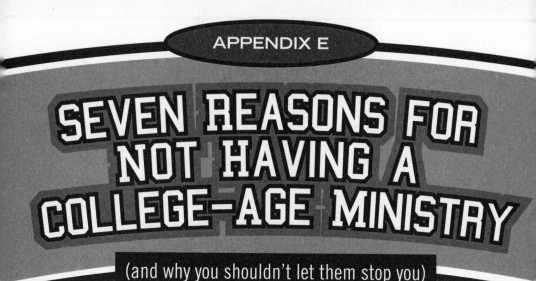

SEVEN REASONS FOR NOT HAVING A COLLEGE-AGE MINISTRY

(and why you shouldn't let them stop you)

I find that leaders of churches that don't currently have a college-age ministry bring up seven common issues. If you're currently facing opposition in your church, then I encourage you to talk about these issues with those who object, or just give them this list that deconstructs the arguments against college-age ministry.

1. A limited number of college-age people are around. When I started doing college-age ministry, all I had to work with was a list of six names. Six. I was certain the need was greater than this short list suggested, so I drove through town to get a sense for how many college-age people were just hanging around. I drove for hours and barely saw any high school students, much less college-age people.

I had no idea why this church had brought me here to start this ministry. But that was my job, so I called those six people and invited them to a barbecue at my house. Nine people showed up. We started a Bible study on Thursday nights, and before we knew it, college-age people were coming from "nowhere." If our growth surprised anyone, it was me.

Not having any college-age people in the church shouldn't deter people from starting a ministry; it should prompt them to start one. How many junior high students would be at your church if you didn't have a junior high ministry?

In the beginning of our ministry, I realized a lot of college-age people were coming from other churches. I was initially concerned about this dynamic and even told people to go back to their churches. But I began to realize the reason they were coming was that we had something specifically for them. Most of the other churches in our area were doing nothing. I heard it all the time: "I come here because I feel like I fit." Or "I come here because there are actually people my age." If we meet them where they are, then they will come.

2. Parachurch organizations will take care of this age group.

The church has largely handed over college-age ministry to para-church organizations—and I'm not proud of this fact. Every major campus has some kind of ministry organization for students—and most of them do fine work as they minister to college-age people. However, they do virtually nothing to help assimilate college-age people back into congregations, which only prolongs the detach-ment they experience. They leave their campus ministry without having been exposed to the positive elements of being connected to the church. They haven't felt the beauty of older, more mature believers investing in them, opening their homes, and caring about their lives.

I'm thankful for these ministries, but if the church had been doing its job, they wouldn't be necessary. The number of para-church organizations for college students should be a wake-up call to church leaders. There's obviously a need—one we've ignored for too long.

3. It will be a financial liability. Let me be clear: I don't like to talk about money, especially in the context of ministry. However, the reality is that finances are a major reason why churches aren't pursuing college-age ministry. And it's true: College-age ministry doesn't really pay for itself the way other ministries do. It may not directly bring in more families or more adults who then give money to the church. But I believe college-age ministry pays for itself, just not *directly*.

In our church, more than 80 percent of our student-ministry volunteers are college-age people. It's no surprise that the stronger these youth ministries are, the more families come. (I only mentioned student ministry here, but children's ministry and others also apply.) When families are present, so are finances. But those college-age volunteers are at our church because of the college-age ministry. The ministry brings them in, they get connected and discipled, and they serve in a ministry that brings in more families. When we invest in college-age people, they reciprocate by investing in the church.

This ministry also pays for itself indirectly because it focuses on assimilation. If there's no college-age ministry, there's not much to keep college-age people involved in the church. And most of them don't come back. What does this scenario have to do with finances? College-age people might not directly bring money into the church during the ages of 18 to 25, but if they stay involved, they're much more likely to continue their church involvement between the ages of 26 and 30. And those are the years when they begin to tithe. In our church, those who've gone through our college-age ministry not only tithe, but also continue to serve. Of course, the point isn't the potential of more giving units; the point is that these people matter. They deserve our time, and finances are simply not a legitimate reason to avoid ministering to them.

4. The church has too many other priorities right now. I think this statement is really code for, "We never really thought about this before." I know many churches operate in a kind of "crisis-management" mode in which they can hardly deal with the issues already on their plates, much less think about adding new ministries to the mix. But I believe college-age ministries can often help ease the stress of some of those other issues. If a church is struggling to keep junior high and high school students engaged, then a college-age ministry can add a sense of a next step for those teenagers, so they have a reason to stay involved instead of detaching. If they know people will be there to walk with them after high school, they're a lot more likely to stick around.

Say a church has a problem with a lack of volunteers. I've seen that college-age people who feel engaged with the church community will happily serve. If the problem is a lack of connection for older people, a college-age ministry creates opportunities for those people to serve as mentors and can bridge the generation gap on both sides. Any church that can't create a needed ministry because it has other priorities needs to take a long, hard look at what those priorities are.

5. The youth pastor is spread too thin. Most full-time—and especially part-time—youth workers could easily be considered overworked, undervalued, and underpaid. But the truth of the matter is, we love the world of students. Student ministry is both what we do and who we are. So with that in mind, I'll introduce a thought that might surprise you, especially coming from a fellow youth worker: Our job descriptions need to expand.

One of the biggest mistakes we make as youth workers is having our hands on every aspect of the ministry. This micromanagement is what robs us of time we could be spending on other areas—such as a college-age ministry. Take a deeper look into the time you spend on things that others can do—even if they can't do them as quickly or as well as you at first. Once we step back for a bit and really look at what we need to do, there's more time than we think.

Yes, adding one more ministry will add more to your workload in some ways. But a college-age ministry can do wonders for your youth ministries. As I said, knowing they'll have support after high school means more to teenagers than they could ever tell you. You'll gain their respect and trust faster than you can imagine. A college-age ministry also brings in the kind of people who make youth groups function—passionate, energetic college-age people who are eager to mentor teenagers. I've also overseen everything from nursery through college-age ministry in our church. This role is a huge responsibility, but I must say I never could have done it without the help of college-age people. Really, everyone wins when you add a college-age ministry to the mix.

I've seen our college-age ministry change our church. Take some time to genuinely invest in college-age people, letting them see how they can be a part of the bigger picture of your church, and the same will happen in your setting.

6. All the students go away to school. I hear this defense all the time, and on the surface it seems like a valid reason for not doing anything. In this situation, it helps to think of your work not as a college-age ministry, but as a ministry to college-age people. It's about making sure college-age people know they're loved, exposing them to the life and body of your church, and walking them through the developmental issues they're facing. This undertaking can happen from a distance—through Facebook, over the phone, through email, with a regular newsletter, with the help of campus visits, and of course, through one-on-one

talks over coffee when they're home on break (see appendix C for more ideas). The idea is to initiate relationships with college-age people and consistently put ourselves in their lives for the purpose of mentorship. Regardless of our ongoing relationship with them, we at least have the obligation of making sure they plug in somewhere else. Just because they're not adding numbers to our church events doesn't mean we drop them. College-age ministry isn't about getting as many people into the church building as possible. It's about showing them the benefits of being a part of the body of Christ.

And of course, no ministry should be insular. Just because the kids who grew up in your church aren't around after high school, that doesn't mean there aren't college-age people in your community who are longing for someone to guide them into maturity. I started with six people. Maybe you'll have four. Maybe you'll have 20. It doesn't really matter. Ministry isn't motivated by numbers. It's motivated by need. And believe me, wherever there's one college-age person, there's a need for loving, patient spiritual mentorship.

7. **We don't see it going anywhere.** Many things about college-age people stand out to me, but at the top of the list is their potential. The secular and political world realizes the potential of people in this stage. Political campaigns concentrate large chunks of their effort on college campuses. They know that major social and political movements have historically happened through the passion of college-age people. Yet few churches see or capitalize on this potential. College-age people are full of passion and idealism. Sometimes they make poor decisions based on those characteristics, but I'd rather help them direct their enthusiasm toward kingdom work than try to inspire enthusiasm where there is none. I've seen college-age people do incredible work in the mission field, in the church, and in their communities, all because

the church believed in them and supported them with a ministry that offered real discipleship and opportunities for engagement.

At its best, college-age ministry builds up the church. It keeps late adolescents involved and interested in the body of Christ. To truly follow the call to make disciples out of all people, we must keep them connected—to the church, to others, and most importantly, to Christ.

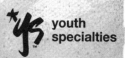

Share Your Thoughts

With the Author: Your comments will be forwarded to
the author when you send them to *zauthor@zondervan.com*.

With Zondervan: Submit your review of this book
by writing to *zreview@zondervan.com*.

Free Online Resources at

www.zondervan.com

Zondervan AuthorTracker: Be notified whenever your favorite
authors publish new books, go on tour, or post an update
about what's happening in their lives at www.zondervan.com/
authortracker.

Daily Bible Verses and Devotions: Enrich your life with daily
Bible verses or devotions that help you start every morning
focused on God. Visit www.zondervan.com/newsletters.

Free Email Publications: Sign up for newsletters on Christian
living, academic resources, church ministry, fiction, children's
resources, and more. Visit www.zondervan.com/newsletters.

Zondervan Bible Search: Find and compare Bible passages in
a variety of translations at www.zondervanbiblesearch.com.

Other Benefits: Register yourself to receive online benefits
like coupons and special offers, or to participate in research.

ZONDERVAN®

ZONDERVAN.com/
AUTHORTRACKER
follow your favorite authors